HIT BRANDS

HIT BRANDS

How music builds value for the world's smartest brands

Daniel M. Jackson
Richard Jankovich
Eric Sheinkop

palgrave
macmillan

First published 2013 by
PALGRAVE MACMILLAN

Palgrave Macmillan in the UK is an imprint of Macmillan Publishers Limited, registered in England, company number 785998, of Houndmills, Basingstoke, Hampshire RG21 6XS.

Palgrave Macmillan in the US is a division of St Martin's Press LLC, 175 Fifth Avenue, New York, NY 10010.

Palgrave Macmillan is the global academic imprint of the above companies and has companies and representatives throughout the world.

Palgrave® and Macmillan® are registered trademarks in the United States, the United Kingdom, Europe and other countries.

ISBN: 978-1-137-27147-1 hardback

This book is printed on paper suitable for recycling and made from fully managed and sustained forest sources. Logging, pulping and manufacturing processes are expected to conform to the environmental regulations of the country of origin.

A catalogue record for this book is available from the British Library.

A catalog record for this book is available from the Library of Congress.

CONTENTS

LIST OF TABLES

LIST OF FIGURES

ACKNOWLEDGEMENTS

My thanks go to the team at Palgrave, our publisher, particularly to Tamsine O'Riordan for her patient and dedicated attention to her work.

Tamsine's predecessor, Stephen Rutt, began the commissioning of this book 10 years after he commissioned my first book, *An Introduction To Sonic Branding*, so I owe him a longstanding debt of gratitude too.

My special thanks to David Marcus, who combined his day job at CORD with extended night-shifts, contributing enormously to the writing of this book.

Final thank-yous to Sara, my wife, for her editing skills and love. And to Jacob and Louis, who don't yet understand what Daddy does for a living but may one day read this book and be enlightened.

Daniel M. Jackson

First, I would like to thank all the inspiring and innovative clients I have worked with over the last 15 years, but especially Jeff and Sara from Sunglass Hut, Tom from Smashburger and Liz from Sephora, who are all featured in the book.

Thanks to all my advisers, friends and peers in both business and academia, particularly my co-authors Daniel Jackson and Eric Sheinkop, but also Bob Finigan, my partner in crime, James Cheung, who has been there since the beginning, Dr C. W. Park from USC and Dr Eddie Clift from Woodbury University for giving me a chance in the world of teaching, our publisher Palgrave Macmillan, anyone who has ever hired me and all my supportive and inspiring colleagues from advertising, music licensing, sonic branding and retail experience design.

And, of course, an eternal debt of gratitude goes to my lovely and wonderful wife, Angela, for always supporting my career no matter how many twists and turns there were (or continue to be).

Richard Jankovich

I would like to start with an official apology to my parents and family for being such a 'determined' child and I promise to spend the rest of my life challenging myself to make you proud.

Thank you to my amazing business partner John Williamson, my right hand Mili Marcetic, my friend and confidant Brandon Smith, and the entire Music Dealers team for working with me and, together, shaping big ideas into reality. Thanks also to my co-authors Richard and Dan.

Thank you to my brother Jonathan for providing more support and encouragement than could be imagined. Many good experiences in my life can be directly connected to you and your efforts. It is an honor to be partners working toward the same goal together.

Grateful thanks to Ira Antelis for mentoring and guiding me from the music industry to the brand side and being a great role model for a (then) 22-year-old, and to Emmanuel Seuge for changing my life by continuing to be patient with my ambitions and passionately championing the vision.

Thanks also to Tara Flocco for the months of tireless research, interviews and editing that led to this book's release. You have helped me accomplish what I simply could not have done without you. I am lucky to benefit from your brilliance.

I am extremely thankful for all of you.

Eric Sheinkop

Chapter 1

INTRODUCTION

BRANDS HAVE CHALLENGES

NESTLED SOMEWHERE IN AN INNOCUOUS office building in a neighborhood wedged between the Upper East Side and Yorkville, just off Manhattan's Central Park, is the financial news and opinion website called 24/7 Wall Street. The reporters for 24/7 Wall Street spend their days publishing opinion pieces on the health of companies, stocks and investment opportunities. These articles get republished all over the web on sites such as MarketWatch, MSNBC, MSN Money, Yahoo! Finance and The Huffington Post. In June 2012, one such article began to ruffle the feathers of those whose job it is to help consumer brands stay relevant to their audience. The article provided a prediction of ten American brands that would fail in 2013. The list included some landmark consumer brands such as American Airlines, Research In Motion (better known for its product, BlackBerry), Avon, Talbots and at least one sports franchise, The Oakland Raiders. The article cites operational issues, changing competitive landscapes and management deficiency as the primary drivers of impending failure. Prior predictions by 24/7 have proved surprisingly accurate.

There exists today an entire industry employing thousands of people whose job it is to help brands maintain a healthy relationship with their customers. We call this industry by lots of names: advertising, marketing, branding. It is a challenging industry as it is, without financial experts predicting your failure. The good news is that consumer brands generally recover from public failures. In 2007, McDonald's launched an ill-advised 'I'd Hit It' tag line, while The Cartoon Network launched a publicity stunt to promote 'Aqua Teen Hunger Force', which resulted in a bomb scare in Boston. Both brands rebounded and today are as relevant as ever. Even Coca-Cola recovered from what is widely considered the single biggest brand failure, the launch of New Coke in 1985. Every healthy brand encounters on a daily basis often staggeringly complex challenges trying to stay relevant to consumers while still turning a profit for their shareholders. Launching a new brand in this cluttered marketplace is even more difficult than maintaining a known entity.

In addition to publicity stunts, advertising slogans and new product launches, brands have hundreds of ways to reach the world across multiple media outlets including social media, online, television, radio, print, apps, retail, outdoor events and more. Attached to many of these initiatives is an audio or musical component – the ever-present indie song in a TV commercial, the background music playing while you shop, the quick audio sequence that aligns with a product's logo (think Intel's chime). Brands will invest in sound and music across their entire marketing and communications platform and are often struggling to know whether they have got it right.

THIS IS A HITS BUSINESS

On average an international brand spends annually somewhere between $10 million and $20 million on music-related rights and licenses. They then multiply that spend by a factor of five through media dollars. This means that a big brand's annual spend, estimated conservatively, is between $50 million and $100 million, specifically allocated to help associate themselves with music and musical talent. How many of those brands become famous for their use of music? How many of them create the kind of value for that investment that their stockholders would want? How many of them create lasting, valuable connections with customers through this music? How many of them have hits?

Put another way, how many of those brands even know the odds for or against success? How many of them have learned how to move those odds in their favor or tried to understand the rules of the game? Have these brands even developed a strategy for using music? If having a hit is a crapshoot, a brand should at least know when and how to roll the dice.

Based on the issuance of ISRC codes (the international standard for identifying music recordings), a reasonable estimate puts the number of new pieces of music released each year at a staggering one million. Each song is written in the earnest belief that they have something to say and can enhance the human condition. If we make a reasonable assumption that around 500,000 artists are involved in these one million tracks then we can easily start to calculate the base chances that any brand–band association will become a 'hit'. We start at 500,000:1 – about the same odds as being dealt a royal flush in poker.

Consider a brand that chooses to use an older, preexisting piece of music rather than a current band or artist's track as part of their music strategy. Our best guess at the total volume of stereo-recorded music in the world is around half a billion tracks. Now stand back in wonder at how any artist's song makes it on an ad and realize that it's not 'selling-out'; it's like winning the lottery, only nowhere near as lucrative.

We know that the chances of having a 'hit' are small to very small, but brands are still willing to roll the dice and take a chance. And there is something to be said for a meaningful connection with music that is neither a hit, nor a failure, but rather a standard part of any brand's portfolio. As long as brands want to use music, it's a moral and commercial imperative for the industry that we represent to help provide some tools; some insight and strategic thinking that will help marketers to cut down the odds to manageable levels. There is no such thing as a certainty but a little bit of clear thinking can certainly make success much more likely. And that's one point of this book. It is not a guarantee for creating brand value through music but it is a playbook, a form-guide and a 'method.' We will lay out a bunch of success stories for you and try to help you move the needle in your favor, whether you are an artist trying to find opportunities or a brand trying to make the right decisions.

Remember, there is no trademark on an idea and what you read here can be stolen and used again. But also remember, there is no guarantee that any of these ideas will work as effectively once you take them and try to make them your own. After all, an idea contributes to maybe 5 percent of the success of a venture, 95 percent is in how you execute it. So, good luck to us all, we'll need it. But before we roll the dice, let's go and learn the rules of the game.

INTRODUCING THE HIT BRAND MODEL

If the game is called Hit Brands then the aim of the game is to create value between the players: consumer brands, customers, musicians and the agencies that connect them together.

Everything we do is aimed at building, adding, banking and spending 'value' in some form or another. Value is not necessarily monetary; though dollar signs certainly help us to keep score. Value is not soft and fluffy either, there always has to be a measure. Value is a combination of practical, emotional and reputational factors that combine to deliver measurable benefits to the business.

In setting out to write this book, the three of us set ourselves the goal of fully defining the complex relationships between music and brands. In doing so, we discovered a model that (to date) has been both specific and general enough to allow us to classify all the case studies we have seen into just three essential categories that together touch all the various components of any brand.

The creation of our model is useful as, now defined, it provides a framework for creating and measuring value. It serves neatly as shorthand for the types of activity that brands undertake, and also enables us as practitioners (albeit with interests in the theoretical) to help the marketing and music industries to talk together positively and with clarity.

This sidesteps us to another reason why this book had to be written. The music industry as defined by its key stakeholders – artists, labels, publishers and distributors – has traditionally viewed the marketing industry, comprising brands and their agencies, as little more than a piggy bank. The view that brand money was somehow 'soft', to be taken and spent as a kind of bonus or subsidy to the 'real' music industry pervaded throughout the late 20th century and into the start of this century. The only thing that has changed in recent years with the demise of physical sales of recorded music, is that the record business (the part of the music industry that used to sell plastic discs to people) has run out of steam so thoroughly that anyone left in that business is not only lucky to have a job but probably smart enough to know that playing nicely with brands is a smart idea. Each of us is on the receiving end every week of hundreds of requests from the music industry on how they can get involved with brands.

So the music industry has had to work out how it can bring value to brands. Not just by way of licensing tracks to commercials, which we could label as the lowest common denominator in the Hit Brand model, but also by moving into truer partnerships, where a brand's ability to distribute music is appreciated, and music's ability to connect with an audience is paramount.

DISTRIBUTION OF WEALTH

Distributors used to be the people who would ship first vinyl, then cassettes, then finally compact discs to retailers. They would physically distribute music to the public through the retail channel while the public, completely in the thrall of the music industry, was utterly addicted to buying and owning recorded songs.

Then everything changed. First with Napster, then with a slew of torrent sites for peer-to-peer file sharing, and now streaming services such as Spotify, Pandora and even iTunes have come along to feed the public's addiction to music to such an extent that they no longer need to buy CDs. People still need to hear music; in fact it is now a ubiquitous accompaniment to every waking moment from the alarm in the morning, to the gym, the commute, shopping, at work and at play. But people don't need to own it any more and certainly don't need to pay anything like the levels they once did for the joy of ownership. We know that music has value in spite of people's reluctance to hand over their cash for a copy.

So the buyers stopped buying, the retailers stopped selling and consequently the distributors stopped distributing. So what? So the people making and recording music lost part of their ability to get heard, to get in front of a buying audience. No longer 'racked' and promoted in store, the music industry had to find new paths to market. Live concerts filled the void, as did a return to old-fashioned radio plugging and as much online and direct-to-consumer activity as they could manage.

While the rest of the music industry was in flux, however, one line of income stayed steady and started to grow. You could call it the

Business to Business (B2B) music industry, which has been a constant and a salvation for many record labels and publishers. It has an intact supply chain, in fact its distribution model is growing all the time. It is a fully functioning market and though it is, forgive the pun, a little 'unsung,' it nonetheless provides the context within which hit brands reside.

FANS MAKE LOUSY NEGOTIATORS

Brands are acting as distributors of music. The money they spend on licenses and the media amplification of the music they choose makes them a serious force for breaking new music, getting it heard and even getting it bought. This is a truth and also an opportunity that some brands are failing to realize while more and more brands are managing to seize. The budgets that successful businesses across industry sectors are putting into the music industry are significant but the value of the assets being created in no way reflects the investment. Why are brands – and we use the term as a shortcut for the marketing and advertising folk who control the budgets – unable to see that they hold the aces? That the music industry does not serve them well and that things could be so much better?

It has always occurred to us, your humble authors, that the B2B market for music is almost wholly irrational, by which we mean there is no globally accepted method for choosing the music for a brand, no globally accepted method for pricing the music for a brand and no globally accepted method for measuring the usefulness of music for a brand. In fact, there is such a complete lack of these things that the conclusion might be that the B2B music market is intentionally irrational, explicitly obtuse and unapologetically illogical. The answer to the question 'How much would it cost?' is invariably 'Whatever they say' and recalls the old joke that, when asked what he does for a living, a music publisher once responded 'I answer the phone.'

Paul Grecco, the Head of Music at JWT in New York describes the B2B industry as indulging in 'random acts of music' and as a 20-year veteran of agencies and record labels, his perspective is insightful. In conversation, he went on to say:

> It is funny the way it [music] works because music happens at the end, it becomes the bastard stepchild in some ways because they have exhausted all their money on the locations and talent and things like that and now we only have so much left so we still have to post mix and color correct and all that other stuff, it suffers in that respect.

All this adds up to music being random and last-minute – and that is the normal state. This persists no matter what the usage is. Slotting music in a commercial happens mere days before airing, choosing an event to sponsor just a week before it occurs or deciding to pipe in music to a store days before opening. In any other business, a process characterized this way would not be tolerated – the market would (or should) move to correct it. But with music the market has failed.

Brands choose music in so many different ways – senior brand people, retail operators, visual merchandising managers, agency creative directors, ad directors, music supervisors and ad producers all get involved. It is then licensed in just as many ways – expertly, inexpertly, from limited-use licensing to 'work-for-hire'. And finally, it is characteristically an incredibly fragmented space in terms of the numbers of businesses involved. There are hundreds of sole practitioners and two-person partnerships whose collective activities dominate the market.

Where the brand industry has consolidated, the music industry has fragmented. There are very few globally recognized businesses in the B2B space outside the major labels and publishers – none of which has managed to create a thriving model for interacting with brands – and while competition can be good, too much of it can lead to starvation or greed; two sides of the same coin.

So why would a market choose irrationality? It probably wouldn't. In the case of music what we can probably see is not a lack of rationality but a lack of education, not so much being intentionally obtuse as covering up an institutional lack of understanding. Brand and ad people simply don't understand the music industry and are not educated in its ways.

WHO OUTSOURCES FUN?

In most areas of business, when an individual does not understand something, such as the law or a balance sheet or logistics, they tend to hire some experts. That's a sensible thing to do. But if there is the potential for a marketing executive to enter a negotiation with a major recording artist for a brand partnership, then who would choose to outsource that opportunity? What executive is honestly going to say 'I don't want to talk to Lady Gaga – let's get someone else to do that'? You might outsource IT but music is fun and nobody outsources or calls in the experts to take all the fun.

And being 'inexpert' is just the start of the irrationality. A major issue arises (and this is so commonplace as to be an almost universal truth) when being a fan of an artist drives the ad agency or marketing department's choices. It's entirely logical of course that any individual wants to meet and work with their music heroes. But it is entirely illogical to let that same person handle negotiations.

It is also true that the nuanced way in which music has traditionally been handled makes it (currently) singularly unsuitable for a separation of the creative from the commercial. Eighty percent of brand music briefs start from a position of 'What is the perfect music?' before moving on to 'Can we afford it?' and, inevitably, 'No, we can't.' The job of the music buyer for advertising invariably becomes characterized by this stream of consciousness and much of the work therefore involves a constant juggling of creativity and cost to find something that sounds like the perfect track but costs about the same as a small family car instead of a Ferrari. Even more controversial, there exists an entire ecosystem of sound-alike music creators who will provide a piece of music that 'feels like' the big hit single of the day.

The final and most damning of all the characteristics of the industry is that the irrational and inexcusable behaviors are covered up through a lack of measurement, evaluation and benchmarking. In failing to measure the efficacy of their music choices, in choosing not to define value or keep score, brands simply enable the next irrational choice and next ineffective negotiation.

The solution to the lack of rational, value-based B2B music is not necessarily to introduce hard-nosed negotiation and remove all the fun out of it. And measurement of value is actually very hard. But we do need to move on from the status quo where brands and agencies largely rely upon entirely the wrong method for choosing music – 'I'm a fan' – and then trust the wrong people – 'fans' – to negotiate the deals.

ADS, DRUGS AND ROCK 'N' ROLL

Professor Steven Pinker wrote:

> Compared with language, vision, social reasoning and physical know-how, music could vanish from our species and the rest of our lifestyle would be virtually unchanged. Music appears to be a pure pleasure technology, a cocktail of recreational drugs that we ingest through the ear to stimulate a mass of pleasure circuits at once.[1]

So perhaps, as the Professor says, music is a recreational drug, not merely an accompaniment. And given the advertising and marketing industry's generally liberal approach to recreational activities it's no surprise that they consume music in rock-star proportions, get hooked on it and end up not thinking straight. And like any recreational activity, music and musical choices are at the same time both utterly inconsequential and incredibly important. This is not the paradox it seems.

Given that there are maybe half a billion pieces already recorded and an infinite possibility exists to record new ones, why is nobody else making the point that any one piece of music chosen, does not have to be the *only* piece a brand could use to have a 'hit'? And if we agree with that statement, then there are surely hundreds of pieces of music that would probably work just as well as the chosen one, so how can it ever be worth paying a premium for one specific choice?

Yet given the *droit d'auteur* or 'right of authorship' that comes from being senior within a brand organization, it is probably not very realistic to think that anyone can really argue against that senior person's right to make a choice based upon their musical taste. Why shouldn't the chief marketing officer's love of Coldplay, Lady Gaga or Katy Perry be indulged? And if they can afford it and are willing to pay for it, then why can't they have it?

We believe that there are ways to rationalize the irrational behaviors of brands toward music. We can argue on both sides about the choices that are made and why, blaming them on fandom or the boss having 'earned the right', but this ignores the damage that they incur. The fact is that an addiction to music and the consequent business decisions made under the influence of these addictions, while seemingly benign, are actually undermining the status of advertising and marketing executives.

Which other key executives can spend hundreds of thousands of dollars on licenses without logic or measurement? They are unquestionably limiting the value being sought and delivered from brand investment in music and they are certainly stunting the growth to maturity of the music industry. The fact remains that while faced with customers who behave irrationally, there is a disincentive for the music industry to put in place the kind of logical trading practices that characterize rational markets.

Does the incentive really exist for the development of a trading currency? Though it is fairly easy to conceive of a simple equation for costing music as a function of its length, its fame and the advertising ratings being bought, nobody has yet tried the kind of cross-industry initiative that could see pricing models developed. Why should the industry go to that bother if the buyers are not asking?

WHO? A CUSTOMER? NO, I CHOSE THIS FOR ME.

If irrationality characterizes the B2B market for music, then it is surely best summed up by considering the fact that while decisions are made B2B, the end user of the recreational drug is neither the music industry nor the brand (and it is least of all the ad agency). The real user and the one for and at whom all music choices should be aimed is the consumer, because brands need music not for music's sake, they need music in order to help them connect on an emotional level with the audiences for their goods or services. It is not, therefore, accurate to consider only a B2B music industry, because the real value chain is business to business to consumer (B2B2C) and only by viewing a brand's musical choices in the context of their consumers can rational choices start to be made.

The notion of customer-centric musical choices is why we rarely criticize a brand that seeks out wildly popular music for its communications. If it is affordable then it is a pretty good idea to associate your brand with the music that is the most popular with your customers. Of course, there are dangers associated with using very popular music for brands; they range from cost, to lack of control of licensing and the likely inability to link the song explicitly to the brand if it is being heard everywhere in every part of the consumer's life. But at least the intention is right in this kind of choice because the business is asking 'What do our customers like and how can we be associated with these things?' That is a good place to start the hit brands journey.

It is also a good place to bring back the concept of value. We must be certain to ask what value brands can bring to their customers through the use of music. More critically, is 'value to customers' really the way to judge whether a brand has had a hit? In almost every way possible the answer to this question is 'yes'. Value to the customer has to be the truest measure of successful branding of any kind, because that value to the customer is what translates into recall, awareness, affinity, loyalty and the love every brand craves from its constituency.

YOU GET WHAT YOU MEASURE

So how do we know if we've had a hit? What is the measurement that speaks most truthfully about value created through music in a branding context? Unfortunately, there's no one method, no single measure, but in this book we want to illustrate a few different ways to judge whether value has been created.

The most direct measure of value is the business's bottom line. How much extra money is in the register at the end of the day? It's rare that anyone in advertising or marketing gets to see these figures and while that holds true for the purveyors of music, there are some places where the right or wrong music has a direct and tangible effect on money in the bank.

This direct music-to-money relationship is easily visible when a brand gets involved in selling music in physical or digital formats. Apple's creation of a music download service certainly ticked every box for its customers and the proof has been that sales via iTunes in

2011 exceeded $6 billion.[2] With Apple we see the ultimate study in how a brand – a technology hardware manufacturer in this case – harnessed the power of music to connect emotionally with an audience and rewrote the playbook for corporations. As much as its focus on design and usability, together with its supply-chain management and intelligent retailing, have contributed to the story, it was the iPod that first put Apple technology into the hands of the mass market. Following this, the iTunes software and music then enabled the brand to build a useful and important place in the day-to-day lives of its customers.

The idea of a brand generating hard currency directly from the sale of music was clearly not original to Apple. Many companies have sought to vertically integrate music into their offering – Sony being another obvious example – and Coca-Cola also pioneered digital download stores in the early 1990s with their MyCokeMusic project, which, although ultimately unsuccessful, was before iTunes the biggest in Europe. The mid to late 90s also saw an explosion of lifestyle brands like Hotel Costes and Buddha Bar transferring their brand value to lines of CDs available for purchase.

So back to our **Hit Brand Music Planning Model**. It is true to say that there are so many brands over the years that have sought to sell music that **music as currency** has formed one of the three major models that we are introducing in this book.

Eric Sheinkop knows as much as anyone about the power of music to directly deliver revenue for a brand. As a founder of Music Dealers he has built an online platform for B2B music sales that has not only become the envy of the industry, but has even tempted Coca-Cola to invest. As he will describe in his own words, music as a hard currency generator is a key strand of the Hit Brands model, but potentially even more important for now and the future is the concept of music as social currency. His ideas in this area, backed by some of the most interesting case studies out there – told from an insider perspective – are in many ways a blueprint for the future of the music and brand relationship.

By way of introduction to the concept of music as social currency, a snapshot of today's social media users reveals that seven of the top eight most followed people on Twitter are in the music business, as shown in Table 1.

Table 1: Top eight Twitter users

User	Followers
Lady Gaga	30,567,050
Justin Bieber	29,309,238
Katy Perry	28,111,938
Rihanna	26,358,990
Britney Spears	21,305,986
Barack Obama	21,239,411
Taylor Swift	19,907,465
Shakira	18,507,525

Source: TwitterCounter.com, as at 24 October 2012

And on YouTube, the top five most viewed of all time is shown in Table 2:

Table 2: Top five most viewed YouTube videos

Video	Views
Psy – 'Gangnam Style'	1,238 m
Lady Gaga – 'Bad Romance'	505 m
Carly Rae Jepsen – 'Call Me Maybe'	391 m
Eminem – 'Not Afraid'	387 m
Pitbull – 'Give Me Everything'	274 m

Source: YouTube.com *Most Viewed Videos, All Time*, as at 25 January 2013

Finally, Table 3 shows the top five celebrities on Facebook.

Table 3: Top five celebrities on Facebook

Celebrity	Fans
Rihanna	62 m
Eminem	62 m
Shakira	55 m
Lady Gaga	53 m
Michael Jackson	52 m

Source: Socialbaker.com/facebook-pages, as at 24 October 2012

These numbers provide hard evidence of the power of music to get people online and engaged through social media. So, given all the discussions taking place, it is little wonder that music as social currency is probably the most important new development for growing hit brands and also for measuring the value of a brand's musical activities. Follows, views, fans and likes are proving to be a legitimate currency for valuing social media activities and point the way to how a brand could truly measure a musical 'hit' in the new economy.

LET'S GET PHYSICAL

The other area where the direct link between music and a brand's income may be seen is in physical environments. Brands have been using music explicitly to engage with their customers in retail and corporate environments for as long as the technology has existed, but the levels of sophistication – particularly through zoning and brand-led musical choices – have improved massively since a company called Muzak first delivered 'elevator music' to soothe the nervously ascending New Yorkers of the 1930s.

Where 'soothing' was the value delivered to listeners in elevators, increases in productivity became the value delivered to management, as music was used in the industrial age to keep employees motivated and engaged. The golden age of music in the physical branded environment could be said to have arrived in the 1980s, as stores became increasingly adept at altering music to affect the flow of human traffic – increasing or decreasing dwell time, for example. McDonald's most famously turned up the volume and beats per minute during busy periods to move people more quickly through the restaurant.

This type of functional or utilitarian use of music has dominated thinking for more than 80 years. Since the turn of the century, however, there has been a massive increase in the level of understanding of how to combine utilitarian music – that soothes or motivates, speeds up or slows down – with the aesthetic use of music that really engages and builds brand affinity.

Companies all over the world have driven forward this combining of utility and aesthetic, and one leading music branding expert, Richard Jankovich, has helped to define the musical aesthetic of major retail, restaurant and hospitality brands across the US. Richard's belief in the power of music branding is evident in his founding of two businesses dedicated to the symmetry of music and brands. First, B(R)ANDS Music Branding Group, Inc., founded in 2008, provides strategy and music branding services to agencies, music providers and consumer brands. Shoplifter In-Store Radio Promotion, launched in early 2013, is focused specifically on helping artists and labels better understand the world of in-store radio and help get their music placed into the hippest retail playlists.

In his section of this book, **Music as engagement**, Richard deals with the physical where the value of music is defined in the cash registers at the end of each day. In this, as in other physical environments, the effect of music is instant, visceral and potentially incredibly powerful. We can all admire how branded environments, such as those created by Abercrombie & Fitch or Hollister, have been tailored and designed to deliver music that appeals enormously to their target customers, and have the boldness to be far too loud to appeal to anyone over a certain age. Music environments are just as crucial for less energetic brands and Richard's belief that all customers, not just the youngest and hippest, deserve an intelligent music experience underscores his writing in this book.

Those musical choices are not accidental, certainly not the random acts of music that characterize advertising choices. They are grounded in a creative and commercial strategy. In Chapter 6, through three recent case studies, Richard gives us an insight into how 'hits' have been achieved and shows exactly how a retail brand may harness the power of music to really engage its audience.

DANCING – NOT SHOPPING

A different but equally interesting take on music as engagement can be seen in the way that brands are increasingly using music as the primary reason to interact with people and then seeking to turn those people into customers. Most obviously, this has been taking place at music festivals, where brands are setting up to engage with new and existing customers, deliver them some value and then attempting to sell them some of their products. The range of branded, commercial opportunities at existing music festivals is very large and we have not yet seen any one method or case study that really stands out.

What does stand out, however, are the case studies where brands have not simply turned up at a festival in order to sell something to someone, but where they have created and invented musical engagements for people that are intrinsically owned by and linked to the brand and its benefits. Of these, the two most notable are T in the Park, a Scottish music festival owned and run for the benefit (and consumption) of Tennent's Lager, and Arthur's Day, an invention of Diageo as a pouring opportunity for its Guinness brand.

While T in the Park is an impressive study in the organic growth of a branded musical engagement, it is not included here as a full case study as it was not designed explicitly from the ground up as a way for Tennent's to engage with their audience. It was more like a great sponsorship that grew with the popularity of music festivals in the UK in the 1990s, no less impressive today but not specifically designed.

Arthur's Day is included as a case study because it is a pure fabrication of the brand – a day in the year made up by Guinness in order to sell more Guinness. And despite or because of the explicit nature of its genesis and existence, it has flourished and grown. It provides a potential blueprint for other brands so there is much to be gained from its study.

TRUE TO BRAND IDENTITY

In 2003 Daniel Jackson wrote *Sonic Branding: An Introduction*,[3] in which, together with Paul Fulberg and a number of branding experts, he set out a blueprint for how to create music and sound identities for brands. As well as examining the history of music and sound – from biblical times to Intel Inside – he sought to describe and codify the 'craft' that practitioners could use to develop sonic branding for themselves.

The legacy of that book is a vibrant and rapidly growing industry based upon those principles. There are now successful sonic branding agencies in every major market and we find that 99 percent of the marketing and advertising people we meet are familiar with the terms, case studies and benefits of the approach. This is a far cry from 1997 when Daniel first started talking about sonic branding and was met with universally blank stares.

From the genesis of the sonic branding industry, the codification of method and the scope of the approach have broadened significantly and today there are people and agencies legitimately describing sonic branding in a diverse range of sectors. Some are focused upon retail environments, some in telephony, digital and highly developed experiential design. The majority, however, are clustered within advertising and marketing. The reasons for this are many but are chiefly based on money and opportunity. First, brands tend to put very significant budgets into these areas, and this obviously attracts vendors. Second, the existing model for ad agencies and interested parties to choose and place music in ads is broken, as discussed earlier, and this has created the opportunity for sonic branding to offer an alternative and viable model.

This model is based upon more objective choices of music based upon brand values and customer needs and it provides a robust business case for musical choices based upon established principles of asset creation and investment.

What it has also done is broadened the scope of what might be termed sonic branding. Where once it meant a jingle or a 'sting', sonic branding today undoubtedly includes any length or type of music that may be used as part of the brand's identity.

In this book, Daniel is taking the opportunity to describe the work undertaken by his company on behalf of Barclaycard – a UK-based global payments business – and NESCAFÉ, the world's number one hot beverage brand. Both cases, with their scale and scope, should provide an understanding of what is possible in the realm of music as identity. From our point of view they describe just how far the industry has come!

AND THIS IS WHERE WE ARE GOING

The model on which we have structured this book states that a brand's involvement in music falls into one of three categories: **identity**, **engagement** and **currency**. By developing this model we are establishing a new paradigm and codifying a new specialism, that of music planning. In advertising and media, the planner is an established member of the team, providing the data and logic that are required to balance the softer creative processes that characterized the *Mad Men* era. In music, the Mad Men only left the building a few years ago and the advent of the music planner – a person in the creative process for a brand who provides robust thinking and long-term strategies in music – is becoming increasingly important.

Firstly, good music planning provides a strategy to underpin creative choices and greatly enhances and accelerates success. Secondly, good planning should extract more value from investments and ensure that money doesn't go to waste – which in turn should secure further funding in the future. Music planning is, therefore, a necessary function both for brands and the music industry.

There is a question, however, about who the music planner should work for. Should they work directly for brands, be part of the advertising industry (like traditional brand planners) or be a function of the record labels and publishers?

We are seeing all possible scenarios currently being played out. Big branding businesses such as Diageo and P&G are beginning to employ heads of music, chiefly from a procurement perspective. Independent agencies are offering the services direct to brands as a 'decoupled' strategic or production service. Ad agency networks themselves are building their own capabilities – with each of the Big Five (Omnicom, WPP, Publicis, IPG and Havas) having at least one of their own network music offerings. Finally, the labels themselves are building a capability to advise brands on how to navigate the waters.

Music planning will probably continue to exist for some time within each of these silos, but the principle of independence will almost certainly separate those who are successful from the rest. The vested interests of the labels and publishers will be a corrupting influence on the need of the planner to do what's right for the brand. It is also likely that the dominance of the creative director will diminish the ability of a planner within an ad agency to be truly brand-centric. It is most likely that in-house and independent will be the right places to be to provide for a brand's needs in music as these situations will provide insight into business strategy at a level above advertising or retail. They will also allow and encourage creative freedom, unshackled by a desire to 'sell' the copyrights in a label or publisher's portfolio.

So the future belongs to the music planner – a person who can understand the complexities of brands and the music industry, and provide compelling and successful strategies that allow them to have a hit. If we have got this book right, then we are offering a toolkit and methodology for a music planner to succeed in the future. And it certainly helps to succeed in the future if you know first how we got where we are.

Chapter 2

THE HISTORY OF MUSIC AND BRAND RELATIONSHIPS

MUSIC IS BIGGER THAN ITSELF

THE HISTORY OF MUSIC AND brands is best described as a palimpsest. The relationships have been written and rewritten many times but the roots are still visible and still inform the present.

In the present field of music and branding, which is extremely vibrant, there are people striving to be the first to launch a new and innovative idea. Whether it is being the first brand to own their own recording studio (Converse's Rubber Tracks in Brooklyn) or the first brand to embed their sonic logo into a pop song (Coca-Cola and K'naan's 'Wavin' Flag'), our peers and colleagues are always clamoring to adopt new technologies and new paradigms for music–brand partnerships.

Every week, technology offers new opportunities for music branding through apps, devices, social networks and traditional formats such as broadcasting, film and events. And when we talk about music branding we are specifically talking about brands using music as a tool in their marketing and communications, whether they are trying to engage with their consumers via free content or to reinforce their brand identity. This idea feels very contemporary but it bears noting that the concept of music branding has its origins long ago.

In fact, if we look at instances where music acts as a vessel for messaging (as it does in, say, commercial jingles) we can look all the way back to Gregorian chant. In 600 AD, Pope Gregory collected and codified all the Catholic chants. The citizens of 600 AD did not sit around and rock out to Gregorian chant on their headphones, rather this music acted as the conduit by which the Church could transmit dogma to its audience. Therefore, Gregorian chant, commonly thought to be the oldest recorded Western music, is also the earliest example we have of music that has messaging embedded within it. People learned these chants and it helped them retain the teachings of the Church while aiding in the spreading of their beliefs.

As the world progresses, we see music adopt many different purposes greater than itself. National anthems become the standard method for countries to drum up patriotism, particularly during times of war or global events such as the Olympic Games. Religious hymns, like Gregorian chant, continue to help the world's religions spread their teaching and beliefs. Lullabies become a vital tool in parenting, with just one single purpose: putting children to sleep. Folk music becomes the easiest way for societies to transmit their stories and folklore down to the younger generations. Music has always been there – pushing our societies forward, providing a soundtrack to our belief systems and the evolution of our cultures.

THE BIRTH OF JINGLES

A quick definition: the word 'jingle' has come to mean lots of different things but ultimately is as simple as 'sung copy'. Strictly speaking, it should rhyme but in reality, it does not have to. It started off referring to a rhyme, then to one that was sung, and it has now become a generic term for any lyrical musical expression by a brand in advertising. But let's go back to where it all began.

In the 1500s and 1600s, the crowded London streets were filled with bustling shops and street yellers. These men and women would stand on the streets and sing short musical quips about the products that were for sale in their shops. These savvy marketers were using music branding tools before we even had brands! Some of these jingles survive as children's nursery rhymes even today. Many of us remember 'Hot Cross Buns', originally a street yeller jingle, and while we may not know exactly what a hot cross bun is, we do know that they are 'one a penny, two a penny'. These street yeller jingles were revolutionary and laid the groundwork for classics like 'I Wish I Were An Oscar Meyer Weiner' or 'Plop Fizz Fizz'.

In 1882, a rat poison company released what just might be the first published commercial jingle. 'Rough On Rats', containing the memorable pop hook 'We give a plan for every man to clear his house', was published as sheet music and was distributed in order that people could sing along on their home piano. Remember, this was a time in American history when every home had a piano instead of a stereo and people bought sheet music to be able to hear the new hits. It is amusing to imagine a roomful of family members listening to this jingle being performed in their living room.

For the first recorded jingle we turn to 'Have You Tried Wheaties?' from 1926. General Mills was close to pulling the poorly performing Wheaties cereal off the shelves, but a savvy marketing manager in Minneapolis commissioned this jingle to fill radio airtime rather than a typical voice-over spot. By the end of the year, they evaluated their sales and found that of the 53,000 cases sold in the US, 30,000 of them were bought in Minneapolis, the only market where the jingle had aired. This offered irrefutable proof that the jingle was an effective marketing tool and started a trend in advertising that still exists today.

In 1944, one commercial jingle leaps from the advertising medium to become a hit song. Chiquita Banana's 'Chiquita Banana Song' transcended the commercial from whence it came and became a fixture on American radio. At one point, the memorable jingle ('Bananas Taste The Best And Are Best For You') was aired 376 times a day on the radio. It's around this time that the golden era of jingles in the US takes off and brings us such classic lyrics as 'Hamm's the Beer Refreshing', 'Nobody Doesn't Like Sarah Lee' and 'Rice-A-Roni, The San Francisco Treat!'

In 1971, the most impactful and lasting commercial jingle hit the airwaves – Coca-Cola's 'I Want To Buy The World A Coke', of course – and this became a worldwide phenomenon. This jingle was so meaningful to Coke's consumers that people began calling radio stations and requesting it. That is an advertiser's dream scenario: free airtime for your jingle. At one point, in the Billboard Top Ten, there were two different versions of the song charting at the same time. The world has seen many jingles since but none as powerful and transcendent as this one, and soon the advertising industry began shifting away from original jingles and toward licensing existing songs in their ads.

APPROPRIATING MUSIC IN ADVERTISING

As already uncovered in 2003 by Daniel M. Jackson's *Sonic Branding: An Introduction*, in 1905 the songwriting team of Gus Edwards and Vincent P. Bryan wrote a song called 'My Merry Oldsmobile' which became a big hit for sheet music and popular artists. The song had the then somewhat risqué line: 'You can go as far as you like with me in my merry Oldsmobile.' By 1908, Oldsmobile began using the song in its marketing as an anthem and in 1927, the Jean Goldkette

Orchestra was invited by General Motors to make an updated recording of the song. What makes this interesting is that it starts a trend of agencies licensing existing songs for their clients.

Through the 1960s, 70s and 80s we see this start to take off, albeit almost always with very popular songs – think Sunkist's 'Good Vibrations' (in the US) or Levi's 'Heard it Through the Grapevine' (in the UK) – but a major milestone occurred in 1999 when Moby released his seminal album 'Play'. Now that may not seem innovative or original upon first glance but it represents a dramatic change in the way brands and the music industry work together. On top of being the top-selling electronica album of all time (10 million copies), 'Play' was unique in that all 18 of the album's songs were licensed to appear in either a commercial, television show, film or video game, many of them even before the album was released. The songs appear in commercials for brands as diverse as Nordstrom, American Express, Nissan, Volkswagen, Baileys Irish Cream and Super Bock Beer. Fatboy Slim's 'You've Come a Long Way Baby', out around the same time, also saw a massive amount of licensing, such as ads for NYSE, *The Virgin Suicides*, the Pittsburgh Steelers and PlayStation. Around this time, we had shows like *Dawson's Creek* telling us where to buy the music we heard on the show, and a real trend where the music industry and the branding and entertainment industries are starting to work together. Commercials also begin to become a new promotional channel for albums.

ARTISTS AND BRANDS BECOME PARTNERS

Brands slowly begin to realize that there is more to the power of music than just the jingle or the commercial license. In an early example of a deep, strategic relationship between an artist and a brand, between 1951 and 1963, Dinah Shore acted as the voice and spokesperson for Chevrolet, which included the unforgettable line 'See the USA in your Chevrolet, America's the Greatest Land of All.' Shore sang 'The Chevy jingle' at the opening and closing of every one of her shows and became synonymous with the brand. During the 2011 Super Bowl, American audiences of a certain age were thrilled to hear the memorable jingle, this time sung by the cast of *Glee*.

In 1981, The Rolling Stones were about to embark on a US tour, but before doing so signed their first tour sponsorship agreement with Jovan Musk. In this deal, Jovan Musk paid $1 million to have their logo appear at the bottom of posters and ticket sales for the tour. This partnership proved fruitful for both parties and so began the tour sponsorship industry. By 1985, pop music and marketing were becoming synonymous and Pepsi released a commercial that was often mistaken for a music video. Michael Jackson's 'You're a Whole New Generation' was set to the tune of 'Billy Jean' and was even more famous for the pyrotechnic error that almost cost Jackson his life. The pay-off for Pepsi was huge and people began calling radio stations to request the Pepsi song, rather than the original single. Marketing and music tie-ins had become the norm by 1986, illustrated so clearly when even *Rolling Stone* magazine began publishing an edition titled 'Marketing Through Music' specifically to track the latest music–brand pairings.

By 2004, when faced with how to release their new single 'Vertigo', U2 decided to premiere the song in an Apple iPod commercial rather than the typical cycle of press, radio and promotions. And by 2008, Groove Armada, a successful European electronica act, decided it no longer even needed a record label, opting instead to release a new recording through Bacardi.

SOUNDTRACKING PHYSICAL SPACES

Something dramatic happened in America in the 1930s. Skyscrapers went up in big cities and people were faced with something new:

elevators that went up 30, 40, 50 stories. Understandably, people were nervous about getting into these metal boxes, so a company called Muzak was born to pipe in relaxing music and soothe these nervous elevator riders. Muzak, founded in 1934, started a revolution of music being provided to businesses, offices and in just about every public and private space. (For two years, Richard Jankovich led the Experience Design Group for Mood Media, the parent company of Muzak.)

By the 1980s it was becoming more usual for stores to have music playing, and by the turn of this century it had become a common business requirement. Brands today have complex audio identities and custom music programs designed to accentuate their brand identity, engage with their target demographic and create a compelling and deliberate environment. Whether a brand such as Abercrombie & Fitch (with its well-known and polarizing retail soundtrack) or a brand such as Sephora (which we will explore in Chapter 6), every major retail or hospitality brand today uses music as a central component of the shopping experience.

CHIMES, IDS, SONIC LOGOS

There is much debate as to when the first sonic logo originated. Television and radio stations had been using station IDs for decades and NBC's three-note sequence is widely considered one of the most successful examples of a branded chime. But in 1994, the entire notion of mnemonics was turned on its head when Intel commissioned the 'Intel bong' from composer Walter Werzowa.

Intel included this five-note audio signature at the end of not just their own commercials but also on any PC that was using their processor. As a result, this sonic logo was heard once every five minutes in its heyday in the late 1990s. Today, sonic logos or stings remain a popular model for linking music and brands, albeit one that may be viewed as 'residual' rather than dominating current thinking or representing the future musical elements of a brand's identity.

WHERE WE ARE TODAY

Today, the music branding (or sonic branding) industry is thriving, made up of consultants, original music composers, music licensing agents, background music companies, lifestyle marketing agencies and the struggling legacy music industry itself, which has created departments devoted to brand partnerships. In 2010, *Billboard* and *Adweek* hosted the first 'Music and Advertising' conference in New York City, which represented a meeting of minds between brands, agents and musicians.

In 1999, when sonic branding was still in its infancy, the agency Sonicbrand conducted a study in which fewer than 10 percent of brands responded that they considered music as part of their branding. A similar study in 2009 by Heartbeats International found that '97% of top global brands think that music can strengthen their brand'. The industry and profile of music for brands has come a long way and today brands seem to be acutely aware of the importance of music across all their various channels.

Customers engage with brands through music in the product itself, while present in retail establishments, while viewing and hearing brand messages in advertisements, while encountering the brand in new environments such as music festivals and concerts and even with on-hold messaging and voicemail systems. Brands invest in music for all these touchpoints but at the moment, they tend to do so in silos. While this is not ideal, it is the reality and the reason why we have split this book into three parts, dealing firstly with music as identity before examining music as engagement in the physical space and music as both hard and social currency.

Chapter 3

MUSIC AS IDENTITY

BY DANIEL M. JACKSON

THROUGHOUT THE HISTORY OF HUMANITY, people have been using music to identify ideas and beliefs, tribes, teams and nations. Music is a natural phenomenon; a unifying love and language with deeper and more emotional meaning than any other, so it must come as no surprise that whenever and wherever a brand seeks to identify itself, music should be at the center of that identity.

This chapter is not the only place to learn about how music forms a part of a brand's identity. It is not the only section of this book that deals with the subject because, semantically, everything a brand ever does with music contributes in some way to its identity. But to make things clear, this section deals in the first instance with the corporate identity of a brand and examines how music lines up alongside colors, shapes, typography and iconography within a brand's register of assets.

CORPORATE IDENTITY

By way of introduction, it is worth laying out what corporate identity really is, what it does and why it is important. Sam Sampson, the branding guru, described corporate identity to me as the first stage of any relationship between a corporation and the consumer. He understood that the core components of an identity are the things the consumer can see or hear, and that the written or spoken name of a brand is the most important element of the corporate identity.

Naming has always been critical to defining a brand. In fact, the *New Oxford English Dictionary* defines a brand as 'a type of product manufactured by a particular company under a particular name'. This rather dry definition of a brand highlights the importance of names and it is fairly clear to see that without one, no brand has an identity. When we are considering music as forming a part of a brand's identity, therefore, we have to consider how and where the brand name fits with the music.

Taking a logical step forward, it's fair to say that any name exists not simply as a metaphysical entity but as a real word that can be written or spoken. The written word has always been the dominant form of corporate identity and, as printing and design have progressed through the years, the visual styles within which the words have been written have become ever more complex and emotionally nuanced.

Myfonts.com, which boldly makes the claim to host the world's largest collection of fonts, has well over 100,000 typefaces freely available. Each of these has a subtle but discernable difference that may be used to convey a distinct emotional driver of a brand when viewed in print or on screen.

There are 2058 different colors defined in the Pantone Goe System. Pantone developed their original system of standardized colors to facilitate the printing industry's desire for consistent reproduction, and today Pantone sets the global standard. We live in a colorful world and I struggle to think of any brand that is solely black and white but even if you can, there are 34 whites and over 70 different blacks from which to choose.

So, here's an amazing equation. For even the simplest brand to express itself visually through printing its single color font, on a single color background, there are 423,536,400,000 possible combinations. That is a staggering number of options, so it is no wonder that most people these days go for a simple sans serif, if only to narrow the choices to something like a manageable number. With too many choices we become paralyzed, which is perhaps why so many brands choose to copy others rather than stand out from the crowd. Helvetica, anyone?

A MARK OF DISTINCTION

If the number of choices within corporate identity have exploded, it is also fair to say that the sheer number of entities seeking an identity has also gone through the roof and into the stratosphere. While the proliferation of brands has been a hot topic since I started in advertising 20 years ago, the truth is that we didn't know how fortunate we were to be in a world where new brands launched every month. Today they launch every hour, in their hundreds, via digital marketplaces and 'app stores' where corporate identity real estate is a small icon, a name, some meta-data and, most critically, user reviews. Very few of these new offerings gain any major recognition and in many respects the app market is a direct descendent of the music industry. There are lots of contenders, very few hits and while every app – just as every artist – has an identity, very few of them could go on to be called brands.

So what is a brand and how does 'being a brand' differ from simply 'having an identity'? This is a topic on which libraries of books have been written, so here is a little synthesis and synopsis. Brands are our emotional responses to the products and services that we are offered and consume. A subtle point here is often lost on the more arrogant executives; the brand's value is ours, as customers and stakeholders. We decide how we feel and despite the whistle-blower Martin Lindstrom claiming we are all being emotionally 'manipulated', it is more a case of the adage that the 'truth will out'. Companies can project their identities onto the world but only their customers can decide what the brand really means to them, how they will react to it and how loyal they want to be.

In this context, a brand's identity is really a small part of the brand as a whole. It is an important part, nonetheless, acting as a signpost to where we can find the brands we love. The identity has the same functional needs as any traditional signpost. It must be clear and point only in one direction. But in our age, when we exist in so many physical and digital dimensions that we can no longer be certain of which way is up or down, just writing the name of a place on a white arrow is no longer enough to differentiate an identity and help us navigate to our chosen brands.

Today signposts use color-coding, symbols (as currently being understood through the practice of 'semiotics') and sounds. Each of these works together to create today's multi-dimensional, multi-sensorial corporate identities. That those identities have taken on third and fourth dimensions is a common-sense response to having access to the rich media environments afforded by technology today. The downside is that an identity 'arms race' has been created, where every brand is seeking to add more and more dimensions to their identity and consequently the cognitive load upon the consumer is increasing massively. Fortunately, our brains seem well set up to process multi-sensory messages and there is plenty of research that tells us that bi-modal visual-auditory sensory experiences in particular are processed very efficiently by two of my favorite parts of the brain – the superior temporal gyrus and intraparietal sulcus.

IT'S NOT BRAIN SURGERY

Anyone who thinks that neuroscience has anything to teach us about how music can create a 'hit' brand identity needs his or her head examined. I've read the books and conducted experiments using brain imaging during listening, but I'm yet to find out anything useful when it comes to creating hit musical identities. What I know about creating hits is what I have learned from experience, which is why Eric, Richard and I have made a conscious decision to focus on case studies of work with which we have been personally involved.

In this section, we have two contrasting cases – NESCAFÉ and Barclaycard – both brands with which I have been deeply and personally involved for some years. The reason these brands have taken up years of my life rather than the few weeks it might take to create a mnemonic or jingle is simple. A 'hit' brand identity in music is not a one-off project. It is an ongoing process of managing the identity of the brand in sound, across time, territory and touchpoint. It encompasses not just the design of musical 'signposts' but the soundtracks to TV commercials, video content, physical devices, apps and any other digital media where sound is enabled and the brand has a presence.

So while this section starts in corporate identity, the reality of **music as identity** is that it relies heavily on a brand's communications – ads and content – to become real, to live and breathe and ultimately to be a 'hit'. So let's be under no illusion, it is the ad agencies that still control the method of creating brand hits. They are trusted with the most critical creative processes that put music into a customer's ears via the media, without whose support musical identities cannot exist. This is why it is such a shame that ad agencies are the last major business area to embrace the music planning approach, the final piece in the jigsaw to support a strategic use of music and the development of musical assets for a brand.

I'LL KNOW IT WHEN I HEAR IT

The worst excesses of the ad industry, the deepest seated issues they have in their lack of process or governance, the basest of their instincts and the greatest of their strengths are summed up in this simple phrase. 'I'll know it when I hear it' has become the greatest cliché of the music–brand relationship with regard to advertising music. Ad agencies have used this truth – we'll all know it when we hear it – to avoid having to engage with the concept of music planning, which is usually deemed to be creatively inhibiting.

Consequently, the last ten years of growth in sonic branding have mainly taken place outside the ad agency, in independent businesses, servicing the brand directly. While this was a shame for the early mover music planning agencies – ad agency support could have really accelerated the growth of ideas – it is now becoming apparent that things are getting better. There is a new cordiality between ad agencies and those with music identity processes, as music has ceased to be a universal joy in the ad process and has become expensive, in terms of both money and time, in relation to other production elements.

More important to this new, peaceful relationship is the advent of musical identities and strategies that are in line with the core associations of building value into brand assets, at the same time showing sympathy to the difficulties of the communications process. Given how mired the advertising process has become in the complexities of the consumer and media landscape, it is still a minor miracle any ad ever sees the light of day. The reliance upon testing and research has arguably gone too far with many major advertisers (arguably not far enough with others) and the difficulty for a creative team to conjure a new line or a new positioning is now greater than it has ever been. It is natural then that any process (such as sonic branding) that removes one level of complexity and delivers the framework for high levels of creativity should begin to be embraced.

WHAT IS A HIT IDENTITY?

The successful signpost is clear and points in one direction. So it is with musical identity. The listener should recognize what they hear, and understand the brand to which the identity refers. All great sonic branding ticks these two boxes and can be measured through two simple questions to listeners: do you recognize this sound? And can you tell us the brand with which it is associated? Hit identities can and should be measured and valued through these foundational research questions. Think of any jingle or mnemonic and it will score really well with these questions.

For a long time in the history of advertising, good recall and a link to the brand were the only measures that mattered – in fact they drove a lot of behaviors that resulted in the overwhelming popularity of the jingle as an advertising trick of the trade. But recall and association, though fundamental, are not the only measures of a hit musical identity. They are simply functional benefits of having a well-designed 'earworm' (from the German *Ohrwurm*) and being able to afford or having access to enough listener impacts to embed the worm in the ear.

The next level of judging a hit has to be aesthetic and emotional. The measure of the emotional impact of the musical identity can best be summed up through the research questions: 'Do you like this music?' and 'What does it make you feel?'

If the answer is that the music is liked and that the feelings are in line with the objectives of the brand, then we start to have something really special – a musical identity that is no longer a signpost, simply pointing at a destination, but is now also a symbol for some of the ideas of the brand. This is much more powerful, as a system of symbols can be used flexibly and can be taken out of context while retaining meaning. Most importantly, musical symbols, just like their graphic equivalent, work perfectly well without syntax. This makes a musical symbol capable of meaning the same thing across the globe, whereas the jingle or sung copy does not travel nearly as well.

When designing the musical identity for brands, I start with the aim of creating a set of musical symbols that are clear, recognizable, have the ability to be inextricably linked to the brand and share the brand's emotional context. This is not a simple task and it is not always understood at the beginning of a process how this varies from developing a functional mnemonic or simply finding a good piece of music for an ad. Given that you're reading this far, you may be interested to understand the difference, so I shall explain a little.

MNEMONICS ARE EASY

Musical mnemonics, of the kind asked for by clients and (in modern times) reluctantly delivered by ad agencies, are empty vessels. They shout 'Remember me!' at the listener but do not, intrinsically, have anything worth remembering. As far as briefs go for the musical identity, 'write me a mnemonic' is entry level – it just about gets you a ticket but don't expect to see the show from way back there in the bleachers.

A mnemonic – a device designed to aid memory – in the context of music usually manifests in one of three ways: a jingle, a sung ad copy or a sting. For the avoidance of doubt, a jingle rhymes, sung ad copy doesn't and a sting has no copy at all. An arch example of a rhyming jingle would be 'For Mash Get Smash' from the UK in the 1970s. Of the hundreds of examples of sung-copy mnemonics, I'd cite 'I'm Loving It' from McDonald's and, finally, Intel Inside is the classic sting. Creating any of these devices is not terribly hard. Being memorable is something that music just 'does' without too much effort. The only real consideration, assuming that the creative has the correct 'craft' as songwriter or composer, is the difficulty in getting a brand's many stakeholders to sign off and agree on the ideal mnemonic. Of course, I am totally in favor of a brand's music or sound being memorable. It's just that I, along with other right-minded thinkers in music planning, believe that the music should do more – that memorability is not the sole aim and purpose.

The future for mnemonics is already here and it is audible in sounds such as the iPhone 'swoosh' that signals an email being sent. You can also read about it in the Barclaycard case study in this book. The next-generation mnemonics work across touchpoints and their main purpose is to signify some kind of function or meaning. In the case of the 'swoosh' it is a successfully sent email; in the case of Barclaycard, a successful payment. Memorability is something inherent in the sounds but it is a secondary concern to the sounds being linked to things that happen in the real or digital worlds. When a sound has utility, it is more easily accepted by the listener – being useful is always a good thing. If a brand can own the sound of a function (as Apple does with a sent email) they may have a serious hit on their hands. Only a few brands are trying to achieve this but innovation has a long nose and we can see it coming!

MUSIC IS EASY

Finding the perfect soundtrack for an ad, or any other singular expression of a brand, is easy – comparatively easy, of course, but the numbers stack up. There are tens of millions of songs available, they're all searchable by lyrics and genres via web platforms, and picking one that will appeal to the majority of stakeholders is not that difficult when compared to what's really hard. So why do communications agencies make such a song and dance about it? Why is music so often a pain point rather than a pure pleasure? Part of the answer is cultural. Agencies view music as relating to a single communication instead of being a part of the brand identity. This is because most brands have not taught their agencies that the development of identity and assets is of paramount importance. If they did, then music would not be leased and returned on an endless cycle but would be commissioned and owned.

Ownership of music is an intrinsic element of building a music identity. You cannot lease or borrow your own corporate identity, which means either brands must start with a clean sheet and commission new compositions and acquire all rights, or they must find pieces of music that are 'ownable'. This is what Nokia did when it created the Nokia tune and then through repeated use of time, territory and touchpoint it built the case for 'owning' the piece through a musical trademark. Nokia stands as one of the few brands in the world to have understood how to develop a musical identity and it continues to lead the industry on consistency and identity management. Its case study is well placed within the music as identity section of this book (see Chapter 4). Even though Nokia has made great efforts through the years to establish music as a part of its brand experience and as currency, its only true hit has been the Nokia tune. But was it an intentional hit or a happy accident?

HIT BRAND IDENTITIES ARE HARD

We are writing this book for people who want to create hits and this section is for those who want hit brand identities. It makes sense, therefore, to include as a case study the biggest hit with which we have been involved. Over 24 months and with enormous input from our client, CORD Worldwide has developed and launched the musical identity for NESCAFÉ. The work has, at the time of writing, launched in more than 30 countries and is well on its way to achieving its aim: to make the NESCAFÉ musical identity the most famous five notes on the planet. That I have personally overseen this work is a matter of pride. That it is successful is down to the team and the method of execution, and I need to be clear and say that nothing about the process was easy. It involves the use of functional and aesthetic sounds and is deeply rooted in the heritage of the brand. It is rapidly developing as an archetype of next-generation music planning, with central ownership and development of assets, together with decentralized ownership of communications and nuance. We hope that in reading this case study you may be inspired to create your own hit identity to rival NESCAFÉ's.

Chapter 4

CASE STUDIES FOR MUSIC AS IDENTITY

BY DANIEL M. JACKSON AND DAVID MARCUS

NESCAFÉ

ALLOW ME TO WAX LYRICAL about a plant that has become so globally and unbelievably important that it warrants a case study all to itself. I'm talking of course about coffee, a substance that a considerable percentage of the globe would consider themselves unable to function without. Every day, approximately 2.25 billion cups of coffee are consumed around the world[1] and yet most of us would be seriously challenged to even identify a coffee tree residing in its natural habitat.

Coffee came to life, so urban legend goes, when an Ethiopian goatherd named Kaldi discovered some new and deceptively abundant trees. These trees, often as tall 30 ft (9 m), bear berries on their branches and it is these precious coffee berries[2] that are the true treasure. Having picked and tasted the berries on offer, Kaldi proclaimed that he was too spirited and unable to sleep and, on informing the local monastery of his findings, a drink was concocted from the berries that subsequently kept the monks alert long into the night. It did not take long for the news of these berries and the effect of their consumption to disperse to neighboring regions. And so began the journey that would in just a few hundred years dramatically impact on the drinking, eating, working and purchasing habits of citizens from all across the world and all demographics.

Now grown and sold across the globe, it was the people of the Arabian Peninsula during the 17th century who became the first to both cultivate and trade the product. For religious reasons the population of this region was, and remains today, largely prohibited from the consumption of alcohol. So as locals began purchasing coffee and experiencing many of the effects of its consumption, its popularity in this region grew rapidly, not least as a substitute for the banned substance of alcohol.[3]

For those early adopters and the modern-day population who enjoy it now, coffee represents something far greater than a warm, dark drink. For those who love it (and we know how many people do) coffee is often the ultimate comfort beverage, one that delivers beyond taste and refreshment and that plays an integral role in the shaping of emotions – from stimulation all the way down the scale to relaxation. The surge in energy originally experienced by Kaldi the goatherd and described as spiritualistic, was in fact (unknown to him) a result of consuming the stimulant of caffeine. A stimulant can be described as a psychoactive drug that induces temporary improvements in either mental or physical function or both. Caffeine is the world's most widely used psychoactive drug and it causes increased neuronal activity that triggers the release of the hormone adrenaline. It is this adrenaline that leads to great, if a little false, improvements in mind and body, most commonly seen as enhanced alertness, awareness, endurance, productivity and motivation.[4]

Such is the psychoactive power of coffee that one does not even need to ingest it in order to reap its full benefits. According to the 25 June 2008 issue of the *Journal of Agricultural and Food Chemistry*, solely a sniff of its aroma is enough to activate several genes in the brain. Following the smelling of this aroma, it is the effect of a sudden increase in awareness that has led to the modern-day idiom of 'wake up and smell the coffee'.[5]

How many times have you tried to set up a meeting or rendezvous, offering to catch up over coffee? This again is not a modern phenomenon. The first coffee houses in the Arabian Peninsula quickly became popular haunts that the locals came to in order to conduct their business as well as social affairs. They also acted as a draw to the area for visitors who often referred to the coffee itself as the 'wine of Araby', another comparison with alcohol. Culturally, of course, since then coffee has become a stimulant, a comfort, a ritual and also, sometimes, a necessary response to a night of over-indulgence.

Coffee's reputation was spreading far and wide after its initial cultivation, and everyone wanted to be in control of both the end product and the supply chain. Outside the Arabian Peninsula, the Dutch were the first to begin growing coffee in what is now known as Indonesia. This initial movement of the product sparked the origins of coffee trees all around the world, particularly in the South American region. Such was the extent and success of this glut, that new countries were established on the back of the industry and it did not take long for the worldwide demand for coffee to lead to it becoming one of the most profitable export crops available to market.[6]

Today, the United States is home to approximately 20,000 coffee shops with combined annual revenue of $10 billion.[7]

Coffee bar chains sell an ambience and a social positioning more than just 'good' coffee. In short, the global coffee chain has gone through a 'latte revolution', where consumers can choose from (and pay dearly for) hundreds of combinations of coffee variety, origin, brewing and grinding methods, flavoring, packaging, social 'content' and ambience.[8]

At the turn of the 20th century, a Japanese-American chemist by the name of Satori Kato, based in Chicago, invented instant coffee. The advances he made enabled people, for the first time, to prepare coffee by just adding hot water. It was George Washington, however, an English chemist living in Guatemala who invented the first mass-produced instant coffee. It came about during his time in South America, when he truly began to understand the product and began a process of experimentation. Under his guidance the first instant coffee was introduced to market in 1909 under the brand name 'Red E Coffee'.

In 1930, Brazil, the world's largest coffee producer, experienced a significant surplus of the commodity and required assistance in preserving their product. Subsequently, the Brazilian government reached out to Switzerland-based NESTLÉ, the world's largest nutrition company.

NESTLÉ was the brainchild of Swiss pharmacist Henri Nestlé. Extremely concerned by the amount of infant mortality as a result of malnutrition, he attempted to create an alternative source of nutrition for children whose mothers were unable to breastfeed. In 1905, NESTLÉ merged with their biggest rivals and not only added several new ranges to their food products (including chocolate) but also spread the company's operating platform globally.[9]

Upon engagement with the Brazilian government's request, under the watchful eye of their coffee specialist Max Morgenthaler, NESTLÉ attempted to create a form of instant coffee that kept the original taste and aroma. On 1 April 1938, NESCAFÉ (a blend of the words 'NESTLÉ' and 'café') was introduced in Switzerland.

NESTLÉ's overall profit plummeted during the Second World War. The conflict, however, reaped a positive effect on the introduction of their newest product, as NESCAFÉ became the staple drink in the rations available to the US military. In fact, American forces played a key role in the brand's development due to their acting in the role of brand ambassadors across Europe. Popularity soared and NESCAFÉ continued in its attempts to push new technological boundaries. In 1965, with the launch of Gold Blend, NESCAFÉ introduced a form of freeze-drying technology that allowed them to create a high-quality soluble coffee that truly incorporated the full aroma and flavor of each coffee bean. You see, it all comes back to the bean.

As a result of the multiple advances made in both production and technology, NESCAFÉ is now used as an umbrella brand for a range of instant coffee products that has hosted close to 40 different variants of the brand to date. And what a brand it is. Every second of every day approximately 5500 cups of NESCAFÉ are consumed around the world.[10]

Today, NESCAFÉ is present in over 180 countries and produces up to 200 television commercials annually with marketing and communications across a variety of other touchpoints. NESCAFÉ has been part of some historic moments in advertising and has produced some of the most famous television commercials and marketing communications of all time.

The home of NESCAFÉ has remained in Vevey, Switzerland, where all key brand decisions are determined. Despite the overall authority residing with this central NESCAFÉ team, it is the individual international markets and the incumbent agencies that play a key role in the day-to-day representation of the brand in marketing and communications.

Music is a hugely powerful tool that can plug emotion into brand communications. The desire of NESCAFÉ, like any other brand, is to increase customer loyalty and become recognized, appreciated and loved. Music and sound can be extremely effective in making connections (particularly on an emotional level) with an audience and help them grow and develop an affinity to the brand. NESCAFÉ has created a number of sound assets over time – none, however, regarded strong enough to stick.

Since it first began advertising the product, NESCAFÉ has not been able to exhibit ONE consistent brand sound during its successful run of delivering communications to its audience.

CORD WorldWide, the music planning and buying agency that was engaged by the brand, encouraged NESCAFÉ to create a sound that its audience would love and over time immediately associate with the brand. CORD's challenge on behalf of the central brand team was for the brand to exhibit a harmony in their audio selections where all the music and sound would pull together in the same direction. The end result: 'La Figura NESCAFÉ', as shown in Figure 1.

La Figura NESCAFÉ

Figure 1: 'La Figura NESCAFÉ' musical notation

'La Figura NESCAFÉ', akin to most other successful sonic logos, contains a melody. Melody is the component of music that is most readily processed by our brains and it merely requires a low level of involvement from the listener to become recognizable and memorable. As a result, this part of the identity is usually at the heart of a successful sonic logo.

CORD's initial engagement with NESCAFÉ was to answer the question 'What should the sound of NESCAFÉ be for the next ten years?' The development and introduction of a successful sonic logo to be used consistently across time, territory and touchpoint was key, but it was not the sole concern. NESCAFÉ is a brand that is steeped in rich tradition. Consequently, it was crucial that the new sound of the brand was representative of an evolution and a bringing together of recognizable elements from NESCAFÉ's music heritage.

In order to define and dictate the musical DNA of NESCAFÉ for the future, it was fundamental to the process that CORD examined and understood the historical sound of the brand.

Over time there have been three pieces of music that have been used somewhat consistently across NESCAFÉ communications. The first of these, 'La Colegiala', was used for the first time in 1985 when it appeared in arguably NESCAFÉ's most famous television commercial named 'Le Train'. During the 1980s this track was used frequently across the brand's television advertising and became a foundational element of the sound of NESCAFÉ. Constructed of a typical Colombian Cumbia that utilizes the offbeat Latin rhythm, this track rapidly became part of the national repertoire in Colombia.

The second piece of music used intermittently by the brand was named 'Embarcadero'. This was first employed on NESCAFÉ's famous 'Father and Son' commercial from 1993. This piece of music builds on the foundations of 'La Colegiala' by combining traditional Latin American rhythms with Western contemporary music styles.

In 1998 NESCAFÉ took the decision to create a global sound. A bespoke composition evolved that incorporated an element of the NESCAFÉ heritage: the Embarcadero figure. The song 'Open Up' was born and the phrase 'Open up, Open up', combined with the Embarcadero figure, quickly became a household track during the 1990s.

Until recently, these three pieces of music were still used across the world in NESCAFÉ communications. Although retaining distinctive hooks and conveying the true values of the brand through music, the full power of these musical assets was never truly harnessed. The analysis of these tracks, however, a part of a brand audit and analysis, allowed CORD to discover key musical elements which would be important to maintain as part of the brand's future sonic identity.

For this reason, the audit and analysis section of the CORD processwas essential before any creative phase. Irrespective of the brand in question, historic explorations can include anything from advertising, telephone hold systems, mobile applications, office music, events and corporate videos. Wherever it may be, we always uncover some heritage within this body of work, even if it is best forgotten. The audit and analysis can often deliver some interesting, remarkable and even breakthrough information. This dive into historical material will uncover a brand's own instinctive approach to sonic branding and the results are used as a reference for the future to ensure a truly consistent approach. While often highlighting inconsistencies, the predominant purpose of this stage is to uncover consistency in a brand's music themes and trends.

Of the 100 television commercials across a range of markets that were analyzed, it was found that 4 percent used 'Embarcadero', 6 percent used 'La Colegiala' and 6 percent also used 'Open Up'. Each asset was individually loved in their own right by the brand and conveyed the correct feelings and emotions. Had these tracks appeared more frequently, it is possible that one or more would have become an anthem for the brand and have been a real hit.

One clear consistency across markets was their use of acoustic guitars, ritual sounds (sounds associated with coffee preparation and drinking) and, most intriguingly, Latin rhythm and percussion.

NESCAFÉ's musical heritage originated from the coffee-rich regions of Colombia and Venezuela (northern South America) and so the most distinctive feature of this music is Cumbia beat as featured in 'La Colegiala'.

Having explored NESCAFÉ's historical use of sound, it was clear there was a strong presence of Latin heritage. The warmth and 'Latin spirit' of the music combined this energetic dotted Cumbia rhythm with live instrumentation of the Colombian region – panpipes, acoustic guitars and Latin percussion. The resulting sound musically, geographically and historically shared its origins with the product, the NESCAFÉ coffee itself.

This deep investigation of historic NESCAFÉ material allowed us to formulate a clear idea as to which musical elements were key to the brand and should be carried forward to the creative phase of the process. The simplest way to exhibit our thinking is in the form of a DNA word cloud. The example in Figure 2 showcases instruments used, as well as adjectives best placed to describe the impact of the music in the NESCAFÉ TV commercials analyzed.

Figure 2: NESCAFÉ TV commercials analyzed

Displaying the separate elements that combine to create marketing communications allows key decision makers to reimmerse themselves in the world of the brand. It also allows them to begin questioning what factors are truly important to the brand and how they should be communicated to relevant markets. For example: is NESCAFÉ conveying the correct emotions to its audience with its current musical selections? Are marketing communications fully expressing the Latin heritage of the brand in sound? Are the instruments used in marketing communications in line with the historical sound of the brand?

Without experience, music is an extremely challenging subject to discuss. CORD WorldWide believes that by allowing key decision makers to examine the sound of their brand, not in music but words, prevents confusion and subjectivity as well as successfully eliminating personal preferences. The uncovering of a brand's sonic heritage can be incredibly powerful for helping these guardians of the brand to realize just how important sonic branding has been for their brand in the past. It also helps them to fully comprehend the power of music and the effect it can have on their future marketing.

As a result of the complexity of the subject, it is essential to formulate clear guidelines. Whether the music is set to be a bespoke composition or a famous piece of existing music selected by a supervisor, having a set of guidelines in place will allow those responsible to make educated decisions. The objective is that by following the creative process a consolidated understanding of the music and sound strategy for the brand is shared across all markets and incumbent agencies. If adhered to correctly, any and all music and sound that accompany the future communications should contain consistent music themes that are true to the DNA of the brand.

Remembering is an intrinsic part of human nature. For a long time people involved in branding have recognized this and have placed the importance of being memorable, both as a brand and in brand communications, near the very top of their priorities. In the context of advertising, memorability refers to the level to which an audience, after exposure to an advert, is able to retain the information presented. The simplest way to ensure that each NESCAFÉ communication contained at least one consistent sound was to create a sonic logo for the brand. A sonic logo is the symbol of a brand in sound. Normally around three to five seconds in length and melodic, a brand must use this short burst of sound consistently across all marketing and advertising communications. The desired effect of this usage is the ingraining of the sound into the mind of the listener. This is referred to as an 'earworm' (originally from the translation of the German word *Ohrwurm*) and represents the experience of having a tune or part of a tune stuck in your head for a sustained period of time. This is what we are looking to achieve when creating a sonic logo, as often the person experiencing the 'earworm' has no idea why the tune has emerged and also has little control over how long it remains there.

For the first time in its history, NESCAFÉ communications would contain a sonic logo. This was an extremely brave step for the brand to take, but one that could have a phenomenal impact on the way its agencies approached future creative work. By now, the importance of building associations between people, sound and brands was clear. At this point, with that importance assured, CORD WorldWide worked alongside NESCAFÉ toward a model of successful sonic branding creation that would enable the brand to communicate its emotional values across time, territory and touchpoint. When designing the sonic logo these were the three filters that were taken into consideration:

1. **Accessible** – The sonic logo must be easily understood by all listeners. If the sound is too complex it is unlikely to become either loved or memorable.
2. **Adaptable** – The sonic logo must be written with flexibility in mind to ensure that it can be adapted over time, territory and touchpoint as well as reorchestrated across multiple genres.
3. **Timeless** – The sonic logo must be able to stand the test of time. The key to longevity is in a strong melody.

It was crucial in the creation of this logo to take into account NESCAFÉ's successful historical musical assets. As a result, we scrutinized the three previous musical assets of the brand against our sonic branding filters.

On completion of a series of musicology reports, it was decided that in order to move forward in the creation of both a sonic logo and a deeper sound strategy, it would be the 'Embarcadero' figure that would be retained. The first of the historical NESCAFÉ musical assets to be eliminated was 'Open Up'. Having only aired for the first time in the late 1990s, this piece of music did not have a great bearing on the brand's musical history. The melody of the chorus, despite its distinctive nature, was also not Latin in feel and thus no longer corresponded to the brand's musical DNA. Keeping close in our minds our sonic branding filters and the information learnt from the audit and analysis phase, it was decided that the Embarcadero figure would be easier to reorchestrate across all genres and was more distinctive and memorable than its counterpart, 'La Colegiala'.

Guidelines have now been created that outline the new music sound strategy for NESCAFÉ. The brand already does a stellar job in picking great music to suit its communications. In the same way that NESCAFÉ uses its visual logo or the red coffee mug across multiple territories, this audio strategy will aid them going forward to bring all their communications together as part of the same NESCAFÉ family. This information is now used as a reference tool by all global markets producing NESCAFÉ marketing communications. In conjunction with 'La Figura NESCAFÉ', the document contains all the strategic, technical and creative information required to create expressions of the brand that are consistent with the identity and thereby relate back to the belief and values of the brand. Creatively, the guidelines describe the sonic language and sonic logo adequately and will ensure that all the music and sound exhibited by NESCAFÉ is not only consistent but also the desired emotional fit with the brand.

'La Figura NESCAFÉ' is representative of an evolution and a bringing together of recognizable elements from NESCAFÉ's musical heritage. The Figura is a modern, flexible and dynamic interpretation of the NESCAFÉ music's DNA. A fusion of Latin rhythm and the Embarcadero notation, this five-note melody allows for flexibility across genre, mood, territory and touchpoint.

With 'La Figura NESCAFÉ' now fully in place and appearing on marketing communications around the world, it would be very simple to say that our task as music advisers and suppliers is complete. The reality is quite the opposite. Successful sonic branding is the creation and *consistent management* of timeless, accessible and adaptable identity and experience, meaning that now NESCAFÉ has a musical asset at its disposal, there are countless other directions in which it can be utilized.

The incorporation of this new sonic identity is no mean feat. NESCAFÉ teams across the globe have welcomed these new elements of the brand with open arms. Every day, companies like CORD WorldWide, and even thousands of individuals, are writing music for brands all over the world. Irrespective of how good or bad these new creations are, their success and the eventual impact they have on the brand truly depends on the cooperation, dedication and satisfaction of the local brand and agency teams. The decentralized nature of NESCAFÉ, which may have originally posed a threat to the success of this strategy, has not proved to be a problem, with all markets responding positively. In this way, the incorporation of 'La Figura NESCAFÉ' into global campaigns could accurately be described as the largest and widest sonic identity rollout ever witnessed.

For the past year, CORD Worldwide has worked alongside the incumbent agencies across multiple territories to incorporate 'La Figura NESCAFÉ' into marketing communications. During this time, we have seen 'La Figura NESCAFE' used in two different ways:

1. **Tag** – Using 'La Figura NESCAFÉ' at the end of communications. This is the traditional role adopted by sonic logos in advertising.

2. **Integration** – Composers have taken 'La Figura NESCAFÉ' and woven the five-note melody throughout a longer piece of music. Markets have already begun creative work on a selection of longer form bespoke compositions which contain 'La Figura NESCAFÉ' woven throughout the pieces. These longer works are not only in line with the newly devised NESCAFÉ sound strategy but also offer an alternative method of incorporating the sonic logo in a more innovative manner, into NESCAFÉ brand marketing communications. This direction represents an extremely modern approach to sonic branding of which NESCAFÉ sits at the forefront.

To date over 40 territories have incorporated 'La Figura NESCAFÉ' into their communications – a phenomenal response to a project that has only been active for the past 12 months.

Sean Murphy, head of the NESCAFÉ brand, was key to the implementation of this new sonic asset and sees this as the start of something extremely exciting for the brand. He said:

Agencies across the World have become familiar with the process of utilizing 'La Figura NESCAFÉ' and adopting the newly developed music guidelines when composing or selecting a track for use in their communications. The creative minds that have already established NESCAFÉ as one of the World's largest global brands instantly acknowledged the tremendous range of creative possibilities available to them following the development of our own distinctive melody. Managing the sound of a brand, like its many other facets, is beautifully complex but our teams around the World, alongside CORD Worldwide, have made a very good start towards establishing 'La Figura NESCAFÉ' as a global asset.

In time, the use of musical guidelines and 'La Figura NESCAFÉ' will dramatically increase overall NESCAFÉ brand consistency and become a soundtrack loved by all those who hear it. Our job now, as

NESCAFÉ's aligned music agency, is to ensure a culture of musical excellence that aids the brand to maintain its past and current success. If the brand and its agencies continue as they have started, it is inevitable that NESCAFÉ will fulfil their aim to make 'La Figura NESCAFÉ' the most famous five notes in the world.

BARCLAYCARD

The year 1966 was not only an important year for football in the UK; it also represented a change and development in the method in which people approached the 'payment moment'. It was in this year that Barclaycard, part of Barclays Retail and Barclays Banking, became the first credit card to be introduced in the UK.

Barclaycard was ahead of the curve and did not face competition in the UK for another six years, when the Access card was introduced. Even today with Europe's utterly saturated credit card market, Barclaycard remains the continent's leading issuer of cards, with 10.4 million customers in the UK alone.

The brand's innovative nature has always been reflected in the way that it has communicated with its audience. As the first credit card to hit UK shores, the first challenge for Barclaycard was to help the public understand the potential benefits and offers that came with using a Barclaycard, in place of the more traditional payment methods. In the early years following its conception, paying for items using a credit card instead of by cash or cheque felt extremely foreign to most consumers, so the brand had a very practical challenge ahead of them. Barclaycard knew that they had to be sure to explain the process in the simplest possible terms. If not there would be a threat of customers not following the necessary instructions and, in turn, not adopting the card as a new means of payment.

The need to explain how to use the card, as well as its functionalities, led to Barclaycard communications relying heavily on text to educate consumers and resulted in the brand often being identified as a 'talking' brand.

During the late 1980s and early 1990s Rowan Atkinson, star of the comedy series *Blackadder* and *Mr Bean*, appeared in a series of Barclaycard commercials playing the role of error-prone spy Richard Latham. This series of brand communications was predominantly centered around Atkinson's comedic displays, with the first commercial showing Latham receiving both a Barclaycard and information on his upcoming mission. In the commercials that followed, the ill-fated spy was accompanied by a protégé called Bough, whose role it was to entertainingly endorse the use of the Barclaycard while flaunting its benefits.

Through these communications, Barclaycard quickly became associated with comedy while still maintaining its presence as a 'talking' brand. While this was successful, it did not leave much room for music to play a significant role. Music of course would be the brand's best shortcut to brand awareness, far more than the entertaining but lengthy use of comedy and wordplay. Barclaycard's use of music was considered on a case-by-case basis: some of the commercials contained music to fit the scene and others didn't. The reason for this was a concern that music would detract from important brand messages and guidance for usage contained within the script.

The brand continued to evolve, providing contactless credit and debit cards to customers. This method enabled customers to both pay for items and withdraw money from terminals without the need to input a pin number or sign a receipt. These innovations, however, did not stop there and in May 2011 Barclaycard partnered with Orange to launch 'Quick Tap', the UK's first contactless mobile phone payments service. This now allowed customers to hover their mobile phone over the contactless readers positioned at tills and make purchases of £15 or under. With approximately 52,000 Barclaycard contactless payment terminals already installed in spaces such Starbucks, Subway and Wembley Arena, this is fast becoming the preferred method of payment for goods priced below that £15 threshold.

The introduction of the contactless payment devices coincided with a change in positioning for the brand. This positional shift acted as the catalyst for Barclaycard to move from its traditional 'copy-led' advertising and become a much more emotion-led brand.

This revelation encouraged brand leaders to make key decisions that would have a great impact on the way in which consumers would view Barclaycard. It was important for the brand to register that any positioning work should not only be relevant to the current climate but also take the future of payments into account. It was the emerging technologies such as digital, mobile and contactless payment that persuaded the brand to adopt a new role in the eyes of consumers. They wanted to be seen as a 'payments organization' rather than a traditional credit card provider. This was a subtle but vital change. Another important decision was taken with regard to the brand's target demographic. The positioning work aided the brand to identify that they should go beyond targeting a specific demographic and instead work at identifying and attracting a specific type of consumer. This helped Barclaycard to focus their efforts and produce products, services and communications that are rooted in customer insight.

With a change in positioning and target consumer base, came a change in the brand's identity. This focused on moving the brand from a very rational space to one that forged an emotional connection with customers. This was all centred on the idea of 'Liberation from Complexity'.

The implementation of this new identity was a real statement of intent, and showcased how the brand intended to change and adapt to the demands of modern society. 'Liberation from Complexity' as a concept carries with it a great deal of emotional connotations. It emerged with marked and considerable differences to the brand's prior communications, which were prose-heavy and whose purpose was to blatantly promote the features, benefits and offers associated with possessing a Barclaycard.

The paradigm shift was not immediate, however, and as the work was going on behind the scenes of the brand, there was a series of Barclaycard commercials on air starring comedy actors Stephen Mangan and Julian Rhind-Tutt. Once again these centered on humour and were extremely popular and well received, achieving huge Audience Appreciation Index (AI) scores. In addition to this, they were incredibly successful in driving business to the brand.

With the new identity waiting in the wings and despite the positive acclaim for the current communications via those commercials, Barclaycard knew that the celebrity and comedy approach could only take them so far. So in order to satisfy its new identity, the brand knew it needed its communications to convey this higher emotional feeling of liberation in very clear terms.

While the brand planned its evolution, it also identified a disruption that was occurring in the market and a change in consumer habits, specifically concerning people's social media activity. Advances in technology, particularly in the payment sector, were also occurring, with customers developing relationships with brands such as Paypal and eBay.

Barclaycard decided to meet this change head-on with its own disruption in the form of a new and specific kind of branding. This was an extraordinarily brave move as it would have been far simpler for the brand to continue down their traditional comedic/celebrity route and make incremental adjustments as and when necessary. Instead, they decided to replace their successful campaign with a route that went in an entirely new direction.

Their new 'Waterslide' television commercial in 2008 still had the charm and humour of their previous commercials, but had moved them away from their reliance on the spoken word to convey their message. 'Waterslide' was an imaginative commercial and a bold first attempt at visually displaying their new brand identity to the rest of the world. The commercial showed an office worker wearing a suit, about to embark on his commute home. Instead of the traditional options of public transport, car or walking, the protagonist boldly strips down to his boxer shorts in the office, then casually struts down the large, open-plan space to a point where he begins his commute via waterslide. With the huge tube passing through a crowded underground station, library and supermarket, the office worker inside glides through the hustle and bustle of the city, relaxed and happy, even having time to purchase a banana. The convenience of this purchase is, of course, completely optimized by the use of his contactless Barclaycard along the way.

This commercial presented a unique and completely different side to the brand and was successful in signifying change in the mind of consumers. Barclaycard was different and, crucially, clearly able to give the consumer a fun and adrenaline-filled life. The commuter's journey home was extremely easy and stress-free in comparison to the journeys of those around him.

The script for this commercial presented a stark difference to the Barclaycard commercials of old because there was very little spoken word, almost none from the character himself. With less focus on the usage benefits of the card itself, this allowed music to play a more prominent role in the commercial. It was vital, however, that with no prose to convey the new brand initiative of 'Liberation from Complexity', the music was able to deliver this emotion.

Music as we know is a universal component used by brands to plug emotion into their marketing communications, but even in our role as strategic music advisers to a brand, we will always remain adamant that the communication itself is paramount. If the music disrupts this (even if the music is great) then no one wins.

In the case of 'Waterslide', the focus of the communication was 'simplicity' and this was largely achieved through the visuals. This was the story of an ordinary male office worker travelling home in a manner that would make everyone stand up and think 'I wish my commute was that effortless'. The track that was chosen enabled Barclaycard to elicit an emotional communication instead of a functional one, which allowed them to truly utilize the power of music to convey the desired brand emotion.

The chosen track for 'Waterslide' was 'Let Your Love Flow', hailing back to 1976 by a band called The Bellamy Brothers, a country act from Florida, that reached number one on the Billboard Hot 100. It was felt that this track not only complemented the visuals perfectly but also translated the exact emotions that Barclaycard was attempting to exhibit. While everyone felt instinctively that they had chosen well, there was some worry that with the brand's efforts to enter the modern world of contactless payments, this track may have been too 'retro'. It was eventually decided, however, that although it was over 30 years old, it worked perfectly with the commercial. For us as music supervisors, this is the Holy Grail – undeniability.

It was not long until the team's decision was proved right, with the commercial and its soundtrack receiving extensive praise. It was not planned for the song to become a 'hit record' but the team were, of course, delighted when Chris Moyles of BBC Radio 1 dedicated a great deal of airtime to it. The track went viral and sparked a flood of online conversations and a subsequent influx of YouTube hits. This exposure led to the track being rereleased into the singles chart – even showcasing a Barclaycard sticker on the CD casing. The track reached number 21 in the UK chart and has since become synonymous with the brand. The positive impact was immediately recognized through an increase in new customers and through the results of their 'front of wallet' behavior.

Following this success, it was abundantly clear that music would now play a huge role in the development of the Barclaycard brand in the modern era. Stepping away from 'wordy' communications, it was imperative that music should help viewers to connect to advertisements on an emotional level.

In 2010, Barclaycard aired their next contactless payments campaign. Using the blueprints from 'Waterslide', BBH created 'Rollercoaster', this time the story of a male leaving an apartment on his morning commute to the office. Again the protagonist feels free and liberated, using the rollercoaster that snakes round buildings and along sidewalks as his mode of transportation. As he goes along he looks down on the bustling streets filled with commuters who are struggling and sidestepping the oncoming rush. So easy is his morning journey that he even has time to stop en route and purchase (using his contactless enabled Barclaycard) an apple and a bottle of water. Again the emotion conveyed is one of joy, simplicity and liberation – all summed up by our protagonist's nonchalant throw of his apple to a nearby co-worker upon entering the office.

The music, as with 'Waterslide', played a significant role in complementing the narrative and communicating the feelings that were inherent to the brand. The selection of this track underwent the same meticulous routine that 'Let Your Love Flow' had previously survived. The success of that track created a platform from which BBH could begin, with the retro element now an integral part of the search process. Once again many tracks were suggested and dismissed before 'More Than A Feeling' by 70s American rock band Boston was eventually selected. This triumphant rock track was the perfect accompaniment to the visuals, which translated beautifully the feelings of freedom and liberation you would experience if you were able to travel to work on a private rollercoaster.

Unlike 'Let Your Love Flow', 'More Than A Feeling' did not re-enter the singles chart. This, however, did not take anything away from what had been a brilliant campaign accompanied by an impeccable music selection.

The success of 'Waterslide' and 'Rollercoaster' as music-centric communications soon led the brand to explore more opportunities around the music industry itself.

In terms of sponsorship, the brand was most famous for its presence in sport – most prominently the Premier League in the UK. At this point in the brand's life, however, a conscious decision was made to move away from sport and to concentrate on the music space.

WHY MUSIC?

Music (unlike sport) is not divisive. Most people at a concert come home happy. At a football match, half the people come home unhappy.

It was important for Barclaycard to move away from its stance as a masculine brand and become slightly 'softer'. A stronger manifestation in the music space allowed for the brand, again unlike sport, to lessen the limitations of any gender skew.

Already involved with the ticketing programme for the Mercury Prize, it was not long before Barclaycard became the main sponsor of the event. Their music activity continued to expand with sponsorship of both the Wireless Festival and the NIA arena in Birmingham – relationships they still maintain today. It has been quite a journey for a brand that previously had no association with music but a transition that has rapidly opened up a previously uncharted audience.

It was incredibly important for Barclaycard's brand to be seen as less macho and altogether more inclusive. This need to appeal across boundaries was extremely pertinent as the brand began making its first strides into the digital world. In its own right, music had already made that move, so it was now time for the brand itself to face the numerous challenges that came with its own entry.

With the introduction of varying contactless devices and electronic payments, the payment moment for the consumer is now smoother, easier and more convenient than ever. With more and more transactions being carried out online, how does one identify with the brand during a transaction moment?

To counter for this loss of physical touch and feel, it was suggested to Barclaycard that sound both could and should begin to play a more prominent role in the payment moment.

The aim of implementing a sound into the contactless payment moment was to functionally and audibly signify a successful transaction made using a Barclaycard. It was also crucial that this sound not only evoked feelings and emotions that were intrinsic to the brand, but that it was also timeless, easy to understand and adaptable across territory and touchpoint. Therefore in order to successfully translate the brand's beliefs, the sound would need to convey a sense of both reassurance and liberation.

In order for CORD to fully comprehend what the make-up of the final sound could be, it was important to educate ourselves in what consumers are used to hearing. Subsequently we performed a deep dive into the psychology of the 'beep', immersing ourselves in the world of beeps, from everyday sounds including supermarket checkouts, to the financial beeps emanating from ATMs and a host of other branded beeps heard on mobile phones and games consoles.

The audit allowed us to analyze where Barclaycard's new sonic brand should 'live' in the congested and convoluted world of beeps and sounds that surround us. Having assessed what consumers would already be familiar with in this space, it was clear that the majority of sounds were far from distinct. Without the accompanying visuals, it was fairly challenging for the layman to separate the 'everyday' beeps.

The sounds of the analyzed financial beeps were likewise not particularly distinct but in fact proved to be slightly more familiar. These sounds, such as the sound of an ATM dispensing cash, were functionally clear but they were generally conveyed without much feeling or emotion.

It was clear that, in stark contrast to the analyzed financial beeps, it was complex sounds rather than simple beeps that characterized the world of branded beeps. In order for Barclaycard to stand out, it was imperative that its sound was distinctive. The ability of these brands to convey emotions meant that a feeling of success was often associated with them. As the aim of the Barclaycard sound was to signify a successful Barclaycard transaction, it was important for the final sound to replicate this feeling. This meant that the sound would need to be not only functional but also emotional.

At this point we needed to research the brand's historical use of sound and music across all touchpoints. This would help us to acknowledge any consistent music, sound, genres and instrumentation used by the brand over time and identify whether this should be carried forward and accounted for in our development of the new sonic logo.

We analyzed material from television advertisements (see Figure 3), mobile games and applications, radio advertisements and on-hold services. Our work confirmed that there was in fact no unifying sound acting as a glue to hold all of the brand's communications together.

The audit process is designed to highlight any consistencies which we may want to carry forward into the creative phase of projects. Likewise it can be incredibly useful for highlighting mass inconsistency. It encouraged Barclaycard to implement the necessary changes in order to create a form of consistency across their market-ing communications.

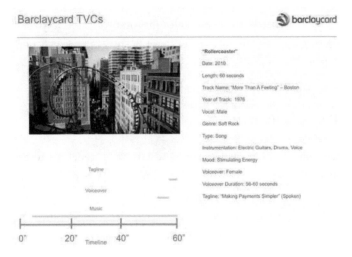

Figure 3: Analysis of Barclaycard's advertising sound

Taking what we had learned from our audits of both the world of beeps and Barclaycard marketing communications, our creative team began the audio mood-board stage of the process.

This iterative procedure allows us to explore the musical representa-tion of the brand's personality. Similar to the process of tearing segments from magazines to conjure inspiration, we search the world of existing music and sound, to discover sounds that 'fit' the brand. This process allows us to identify any specific styles or genres or even a certain pace, rhythm or instrumentation that could be inherent to the brand's DNA.

The first iteration could contain up to 25 short clips of music or sound that are mapped on a board to match key words associated with the brand.

This tool allowed Barclaycard to both vote and give feedback on the sound clips immediately, for analysis by CORD. Clips that did not receive good feedback were eliminated from the process, while the preferred tracks remained and were used as guidelines in the search for further examples.

This process was repeated once more until there remained a small group of tracks that truly represented the sound of Barclaycard. Using these tracks as inspiration, we set about the task of fusing seemingly familiar elements that would combine to create something new, surprising and inspiring.

THE NEW APPROACH
Background

Based on the brand personality and customer benefit – to liberate people from complexity – the sound should make the listener feel that Barclaycard has helped make their life easier and that the simplicity of things that 'just work' is freely available via them.

Technical spec

- A piece of music lasting 1.5–2 seconds: ensure it is memorable but not annoying or self-indulgent.
- 3- or 4-note melody. After exploration, this is felt to be the right amount of notes for the sonic to feel distinct and simple.
- Medium to fast tempo, with inventive sounds and in a major key, to create a distinct and positive sound.

From here we cast our net far and wide and began working with composers all over the world to create the new Barclaycard sonic logo. They were provided with our guidelines, the reference tracks from the moodboard phase and a brilliant animatic. The movement of the animatic was also something to take into account when composing the music that would accompany it. It is always far easier for a composer to work with a picture than without.

The composition phase (much like the moodboard process) was iterative. In total we created and listened to approximately 100 separate logos.

Having played a selection of these to Barclaycard, the concepts that were not enjoyed were ignored and scrapped, while those that were liked continued to evolve.

Once this process had been repeated a number of times, all that remained were three preferred routes for the sonic logo. These three options were then put forward for consumer research, which would play an important role in the final decision.

Taking the consumer research into account, key Barclaycard stakeholders made their decision, and the new Barclaycard sonic logo was born. Now each time somebody used his or her contactless Barclaycard or mobile phone to pay for an item, this sound signified that a successful Barclaycard transaction had occurred. In addition, this new sonic asset would be integrated into the brand's marketing communications.

Now that the development of the sonic logo was complete, it allowed for the exploration of other areas where Barclaycard could improve its use of music and sound. As previously mentioned, Barclaycard was extremely successful in choosing individual tracks to accompany specific communications. This led to a number of fantastic music-centric television commercials. Yet again, however, there appeared to be nothing in a musical sense that united them or connected them to any other Barclaycard communications.

CORD helped the brand to construct a set of musical guidelines for the selection of music in their communications. The brand and those tasked with sourcing music for new communications (existing or newly composed) were now fully equipped with the tools to make their decisions. The guidelines would not only guarantee the use of high quality sound on all future Barclaycard communications, but more importantly safeguard a clear form for all of the brand's future marketing communications.

Since the completion of this project we have worked alongside the brand to use its new sound asset and guidelines in the correct manner. The brand has already used its new 'Open World' sonic logo on a number of mobile phone applications – featuring a great deal on multiple mobile applications, on its on-hold account servicing system, and is in the process of integrating it in various manifestations into digital campaigns, its website and above-the-line communications.

Barclaycard may be a card provider, but its appearance now goes beyond the visual rectangular piece of plastic with which we are all familiar. It may not be long before you forget what it was like to experience this brand in just a traditional plastic format, but as with all hit brands, you will always be able to hear it.

NOKIA

Around the world the Nokia ringtone is heard nearly 1 billion times per day. This tune was introduced onto Nokia handsets for the first time in 1994 and is still present today as each Nokia phone's default ringtone. One may argue that the figure of 1 billion has simply been plucked out of thin air to drum up excitement and further aid brand recognition. Tapio Hakanen, Head of Sound and Visual Content, has developed a simple formula for validating this figure using the brand's consumer research data:

1. Currently there are 1.3 billion people using a Nokia handset.
2. On average a person's mobile phone rings seven times per day.
3. Research shows that approximately 10 percent of people with Nokia handsets do not change their ringtone post-purchase and continue with the default setting.

$$(10\% \text{ of } 1.3 \text{ billion}) \times 7 = 910 \text{ million}$$

OK, so it isn't quite 1 billion times per day, but this figure ranks the Nokia ringtone as one of the most heard sounds on the planet.

Unbeknown to most, the Nokia ringtone is actually a short phrase taken from a track named 'Gran Vals' by Spanish guitar player Francisco Tárrega. It was this track that was used to accompany Nokia's first television commercial in 1993 and was used consistently across all brand communications for the next year.

In choosing this track for its first above-the-line campaign, Nokia made the conscious decision to try and move away from its competitors. At that time, most technology companies were exhibiting a sound that Tapio Hakanen accurately and somewhat amusingly described as 'Feel-Good Business Rock'. From its inception, Nokia has prided itself on being a brand for and of the people. To further demonstrate this, the tagline both seen and heard in many Nokia brand communications over time has been 'Nokia – Connecting People' (see Figure 4). It was for this reason that 'Grand Vals', a human-sounding track played on acoustic guitar, was selected for the campaign in 1993.

Figure 4: Nokia logo

From where we are now, Nokia seems to have been a fair distance ahead of the curve in its efforts to appear and sound more human.

Modern-day campaigns for technology brands are visually hi-tech and crowded with as many aesthetically pleasing images of enhanced equipment as possible. More often than not, however, they are accompanied by what is an extremely and increasingly familiar human sound.

Possibly the most obvious example of this is Apple's use of music and sound on their communications. Without using the same piece of music across various campaigns or the creation of a mnemonic that is used consistently, the brand has developed a 'house style'. Despite Apple's clear technical prowess, this house style generally does not reflect this and, instead, an acoustic and folk sound conveying very human characteristics is exhibited. If the visual elements of the brand are purposely constructed and marketed to convince us of the brand's technical superiority, Apple's use of the Chilly Gonzalez track 'Never Stop' (among others) is a clear example of its desire to maintain a close relationship with its fans, consumers and people in general.

The adoption of this more human sound by technology brands may never have occurred if Nokia had not used Francisco Tárrega's track in their advertising. More crucial, however, to the immediate popularity of this track was its inclusion on the handsets themselves. Today, the ability of a device to play music and sound of the highest quality is imperative. It is quite hard to fathom that it was not until the beginning of the 1990s that this technology was created, with Nokia being the first handset manufacturer to experiment with its functionality.

The first version of the Nokia tune in a handset was a monophonic 'buzzer tone'. Nokia then began experimenting with the idea of polyphonic handsets. When it was clear that these initial developments would change the future relationship between mobile handsets and sound, Nokia dedicated time, energy and expertise to this quest for innovation.

The man behind this technology was Thomas Dolby. Born Thomas Robertson, he adopted the stage name of Thomas Dolby after being given it as a nickname by friends in his teenage years. Robertson was never too far away keyboards and tapes, most of which came from the Dolby Laboratories. His friends picked up on his fascination with these tools and quickly began to call him 'Dolby'. Dolby followed his passion for music and began releasing pop records incorporating electronic instrumentation in the early 1980s. Though he never had many hits, Dolby became one of the most recognizable figures of the synth pop movement of early 80s new wave.

Dolby says: 'At the beginning of the 90s I was getting pretty jaded with the music business…So I went to Silicon Valley, which was very exciting, and for the first time computer companies were starting to take music seriously.'[11]

It was at the beginning of this journey in California where Dolby set up a company that created 'polyphonic' virtual synthesizers. This software not only allowed devices to play musical notes, but more importantly possessed the ability to produce multiple sounds simultaneously.

The Nokia tune was already famous from its appearance in advertisements in the form of an audio logo. Dolby's initial engagement with the brand was to work on an updated version of this tune in order to produce an updated polyphonic ringtone version.

Soon after the millennium, this feat was achieved, and a polyphonic version of the 1902 track 'Grand Vals' by Spanish classical musician Francisco Tárrega appeared on Nokia devices as the default ringtone.

Dolby's synthesizer was a phenomenal invention, ahead of its time, that transformed the relation between technology and audio forever. His synthesizer (which has undergone constant development since its first use) has been adapted to fit almost any piece of technology and could almost be termed the world's most purchased musical instrument.

The presence and familiarity of the Nokia ringtone in modern life could have been very different, however, if Nokia had not been ahead of the curve.

Nokia has always placed great importance on the sound exhibited by its brand, which is evidenced by the decade-long presence of a specifically designated sound team at the brand's headquarters. This team is responsible for the overall sound of the brand, and Tapio Hakanen breaks it down into three simple sectors:

1. All device sounds, including ringtones, applications, pre-loaded music, user interface sounds and the phone's camera.
2. Marketing and communications.
3. Events – most recently Nokia World and the Mobile Congress.

The world of brands is an extremely noisy place. The majority of the sound, however, is not functional or at times even intentional. Technology brands, and in particular the brands among these that have developed mobile handsets, have been extremely sensible in intentionally producing and implementing functional sounds in their devices.

As with the Apple 'swoosh', when a sound accompanies an aesthetic, it helps the user to identify that an action has been completed so that they can move on to the next part of the user journey.

Each time a new handset is released, new sounds are featured in order to satisfy a specific function and/or action. Not all audio is new, however, with Nokia keen to add a sense of continuity to the sound experience during the customer journey. Nokia pays attention to considerable feedback collated from previous handsets and builds on this in its delivery of newly released material. The most effective of these can be seen when the aesthetic of the sound is in sync with its functionality. Apple's choice of a 'swoosh' rather than a generic beep or bong confirms to the user that not only has their email been sent, but that this action has been done swiftly.

Likewise, Nokia has paid a great deal of attention to ensure that the sounds and music present on their devices not only hold a function in line with its aesthetic, but also effectively complement the additional aspects of the phone.

These additional aspects can again be split into three equally important sectors. The Nokia sound department will work alongside these three core teams to ensure that the sounds created are in line with the product and the brand itself. The relationship and continued teamwork between these departments play an extremely influential role in the final sound and music that will be heard on Nokia devices, through marketing, communications and at Nokia events.

THE THREE TEAMS

1. **Industrial design**

   This team will be questioned by the sound department about what is currently driving their work. For example, in 2011 the design principles of all Nokia devices were based around the idea of 'reduction'. The design of the phone was about simplicity. Detailed information around the design of the future product provides those entrusted with the sound of the device with the inspiration and knowledge to create the correct sounds to match.

2. **Brand team**

   At the heart of a brand's marketing and communications is the 'positioning' of the brand. What is the essence of the brand? What are its key characteristics? What is the brand promising to deliver to its consumers at that particular time on that particular touchpoint? Sound and music have an immense power to move people emotionally. Any music or sound used across any touchpoint should align with the overall goals of the brand and create an immersive and rewarding user experience. In order to achieve the ultimate effect, the selected sound should work coherently with the visuals, function and/or atmosphere, creating a seamless link between the two. It is for these reasons that the Nokia sound team fully immerse themselves in the overall positioning of the brand before embarking on the creation of any sound elements.

3. **Digital user experience team**

   As previously mentioned, the best device sounds are the ones where the aesthetic is in line with its specific function. Revised formats of the user experience come in waves as and when relevant. These updates could include advances in: device start-up and shut-down, messaging, calendar, alarms and applications. The sound team must be fully educated in the recent developments in order to identify the perfect sound to match the new and improved format, as can be easily seen when comparing the sounds exhibited by functions on Nokia phones in 2005 with the sounds of the most recent device. The contemporary versions of the sound accompanying these functions are far less complicated and are in keeping with the modern, reduced visual style of the handset and operating system.

Nokia's first phone was launched in 1984 weighing in at a little over 11 pounds. It was revolutionary for its time. In 2005 the company introduced its first line of multimedia smartphones and in 2011 introduced the first Microsoft Windows phone handsets when the Nokia Lumia range was released on the market.

With a new partnership, and the operating system reverting to that of Microsoft, how would this affect the visual and sound elements of the Nokia handsets?

Tapio Hakanen explained that it would only further enhance the position of the sound team at Nokia. He said: 'Now everything is run on Windows, the audio identity is even more important.'

He went on to explain that this relationship was made significantly easier by the fact that Microsoft's approach to sound is very similar to that of Nokia's. Not only are the two global giants extremely close in terms of their approach, but they are also not worlds apart in their sense of style and views on aesthetics.

Simplicity, purity and humanity play a key role in the design of both visual and sound elements for Nokia – Microsoft adopts the same stance.

In the technology industry, there are developments made not only every day but every minute. For a brand to have a presence as long and as successful as Nokia's it must have been doing something right.

Figure 5 shows the sheer amount of changes the Nokia handset has undergone over time. This illustrates changes in visual design, innovation in applications and the implementation over the years of new technologies.

I guess the point I am trying to make here is that since 1984 the Nokia handset has changed dramatically almost year on year.

Crucially two elements have remained throughout – the brand's name and its audio identity.

Audio branding can be developed, understood and appreciated by consumers fairly easily. There are three ways in which any brand can formulate a successful audio identity – Nokia has followed this route extremely closely and has ultimately realized its benefits. Nokia was early to identify that the use of a consistent sound that was in line with the brand's overall positioning and identity would be a strong asset for them. Not surprisingly, they stuck with it! In using the techniques below, the brand has managed to create one of the most famous pieces of music ever to be associated with a brand.

Figure 5: The changing face of a Nokia phone

The three key techniques the brand operated in order to create a successful audio identity are as follows:

Frequency – this relates to how often one can hear this sound. Incorporating the music from their advertising into their devices as a ringtone and later on as a start-up sound ensured that the Nokia sound would be heard frequently. Simply put, consistency over territory and touchpoint.

Recency – in order to remain in the mind of listeners, a brand should ensure that its sonic identity is used consistently over not only territory and touchpoint but also time. Recognition and familiarity are key to creating a sonic identity for a brand. Nokia has achieved this by sticking with the same core melody as the original theme tune.

Relevancy – the world of branded sounds is extremely busy. In order to stick in the mind of the consumer, a brand's sonic identity must not only be distinctive but also match the product it is accompanying. The sonic identity of a brand must be flexible enough so it can be adapted over time to keep pace with developments in technology and society. Nokia has adapted the original melody on numerous occasions in order to work alongside new handsets and marketing campaigns.

The Nokia ringtone was first implemented on the Nokia 2110 in 1994 and has now been modified eight times in order to keep pace with developments in other areas of the brand and the handset. The latest version can be heard on Nokia's 2011 N9 handset. Creative development does not stop at Nokia. Another new version of the Nokia Tune will be launched alongside the 2013 range of Nokia's Windows phones.

Since the emergence of BlackBerry and Apple's iPhone, Nokia sales have taken a hit. Their sales team always has one sure-fire way of identifying whether those around them have Nokias. It is an inside joke at Nokia that sales data is often collected by the team when landing by airplane. How do they know how many people on the plane are in possession of a Nokia handset? Because they hear the short phrase taken from Francisco Tárrega's 'Grand Vals' when impatient passengers switch on their mobile phones as soon as the aircraft hits the ground – or, as Nokia employees refer to it, 'The Sound of Market Share'.

Chapter 5

MUSIC AS ENGAGEMENT

BY RICHARD JANKOVICH

MUSIC IS UNIVERSAL

IN OUR EARLIER CHAPTER DOCUMENTING the history of music branding, we touched on the physical location of retail, restaurant and hospitality brands and referenced the work I have done in the space. In this chapter, we are going to dive deep into this area and discuss the fundamentals of how brands can use music to really engage with their audience. It doesn't take a mountain of research to know that music, like all emotive art forms, engages and touches its audience. Music has a unique power to captivate people on an emotional and psychological level – we all have a song from our childhood that invokes nostalgia and fills our eyes with tears of memory. I can't predict what would affect you personally, but I guarantee that there is one song that if you heard it right now, it would transport you somewhere else. Maybe your first kiss? Your wedding dance? The day your child was born? And though we all know this instinctively, it does help to look at research which underscores our anecdotal point-of-view.

To start, we need to recognize that the power of music is an absolutely universal human quality. In a 2009 study[1] by the Max Planck Institute, this was made resoundingly clear. A group of Mafa farmers from Cameroon, Africa and a group of German citizens were selected to determine whether they felt music in the same way. These two groups of people experienced very different lives – different technology, cultures, religions, geographies and family structures. Both groups were played identical pieces of music and then asked to identify emotion within the passages – to classify each piece of music as happy, sad or fearful. Despite having no shared cultural touchpoints or societal similarities, they both identified the same emotions within the same pieces. This points to a truly universal ability of human beings to distinguish emotions within music. This is one of the reasons I founded Shoplifter In-Store Radio Promotion. The music industry is just as interested as brands in understanding consumer shopping behavior. When a consumer is shopping and hears a song that grabs their ears, they often pull out their smartphone, launch an app like Shazam and identify the song. This is a quick and easy form of fan acquisition for artists and labels. I've spoken with many record labels who are eager for these consumers to hear their releases while they are shopping at malls, eating at restaurants, lounging at high-end hotels or browsing at edgy boutiques. Both labels and artists believe in the promotional value of in-store radio, an audience estimated to be over 200 million people every day, but they are often confronted with the complexity of managing relationships with over 60 in-store providers and the hundreds of individual music programmers. Shoplifter was founded to offer a single point-of-entry for the music industry to the entire retail soundscape of North America.

As Eric Sheinkop points out in Chapter 7, music consumption patterns have changed dramatically in the last decade. When music files switched from physical (CD) to digital, all hell broke loose. Every day, we read articles about how the music business is declining and, in fact, according to Forrester Research,[2] total revenue from US music sales plunged from $14.6 billion in 1999 to $6.3 billion in 2009. This 50 percent drop in value obscures the fact that collections and consumption is rising, as is music's importance and its role in our lives. We define ourselves through the music on our iPods, our Spotify playlists, our vinyl record collections, our auto-populated 'So-and-so just listened to…' status updates on Facebook. How can we better understand the importance of music to consumers if they are no longer willing to pay for it?

To answer that, let's look at some recent studies demonstrating that music is the single most engaging art, media or entertainment form on the planet. In 2009, MidemNet and Music Matters conducted a survey[3] to better understand music consumption around the world. They surveyed 8500 individuals across 13 different markets (including China, Brazil, the United States, the UK, France, India, Australia, Canada and more). Sixty-three percent of respondents consider themselves to be PASSIONATE about music. That is an extraordinary two-thirds of the entire population of the Earth! This is in comparison to only 6 percent who indicated that they DO NOT CARE about music.

Similarly, the Youth and Music Survey of 2009[4] from Marrakesh Records and Human Capital explored the importance of music among British 15–24 year-olds. They found that even though these young adults are unwilling to pay for music, it is still vital to their everyday lives. Sixty percent would rather go without sex than music for a week. Similarly, the 2007 Brandamp study[5] from Millward Brown showed that music is the medium that people would least like to live without (beating the internet, film, books and TV). In the same study, 85 percent felt that music changes their mood. So, we start to see that people value music even though they do not wish to pay for it.

And just as much as people love music, they avoid ads. A recently conducted survey[6] by the National Institute for Consumer Research (SIFO) showed that 75 percent of people actively avoid advertising, whether it is on TV, internet or radio. This means people are recording their shows, avoiding banner ads and changing the radio dial during a commercial. If you are an advertiser with a $300 million ad budget, it should cause alarm to know that $225 million of that ad buy is being actively avoided. Using the right music in your ads is one way to engage people and Dan's previous chapters and case studies point to some pretty successful examples. But when we look at the retail level and online social media channels, we find that music offers other compelling and impactful ways of keeping your customers engaged.

The first retail-focused, content campaign I worked on was in 2007 for Adidas and their 'Music Is Me' campaign. They wanted to launch a mobile campaign to reach their target demographic with marketing around the Superstar line of shoes being featured in their Adidas Originals stores. To underscore 'originality' we were asked by their technology provider to identify ten emerging artists who were eager to be involved with such a prestigious brand. I selected and licensed music, pictures and video content from the artists that would be given away free to customers. Each customer would be prompted via in-store signage to text if they wanted the content. The text would prompt the customer to land on a microsite in which each artist was profiled and their content was available for free download. We saw great success from the campaign with hundreds of thousands of downloads and an impressive amount of customers opting in for future communications. For me, the numbers only reinforced what we already suspected – that giving customers content that is unique and focused on their individuality is a powerful way to engage them at the retail level. I have since overseen or executed similar retail-related content campaigns for clients as diverse as John Varvatos, Texas Roadhouse, The Standard Hotel, Qdoba and more.

I have often understood that music had an impact on a brand's shopping environment from my work experience along with these studies, but I also wanted original research to prove it. I worked with a major, global telecommunications giant to uncover the true value of a strategic brand soundtrack. In January 2012, qualitative and quantitative research was conducted in a variety of stores across different markets in the United States including Atlanta, New York, Dallas, Chicago and Los Angeles. Over two consecutive days, each individual store was tested with the branded music on and off. From 600 quantitative surveys and 80 shop-alongs, we observed trends in traffic patterns, product and staff interactions and the length of time customers spent in store. In all conversations, we questioned shoppers about the reason for their visit, their satisfaction with the store experience, their reactions to the environment and opinions on the music, or lack thereof. We found that music plays an important role in the store experience – both blatant and subtle – and is a particular driver of energy. Prerecruited interviewees described the store when music was present as upbeat and energetic, even during slow times. They even used the brand's own attributes ('welcoming', for example) to describe the store, which proved that our soundtrack was successfully underscoring their brand. When music was not present, they described the store as quiet and slow.

Beyond energy, music was shown to create a 'sound shroud' to help dampen other customer and employee interactions. Music diffused unpleasant interactions with employees and even minimized perceived wait time. On the days when music was present, customers appeared to be more relaxed and move more freely about the store. They were also more likely to browse and pick up products, even after their transaction was complete. One customer was quoted as saying 'I want music when I am looking at gadgets'.

Perhaps most interesting, the shopping experience was considered to be three times more enjoyable for customers in stores that had the branded music. This supports the idea that music is essential to a productive and pleasant store environment and we would always recommend the presence of music to enhance a customer experience.

Dr Oliver Sacks, the well-known author and professor of neurology at the NYU School of Medicine, has published several books that discuss the power that music can have on those afflicted with a host of ailments. His research shows that music can help those coping with debilitating conditions, in particular head trauma. His work is admirable and he is a bit of a rock star in our world, but I often have trouble connecting his work to our sphere of brand–consumer relationships. So I was particularly intrigued when, discussing *Musicophilia*, the *New York Times* bestseller he released in 2007, he wrote:

> Music can move us to the heights or depths of emotion. It can persuade us to buy something, or remind us of our first date. It can lift us out of depression when nothing else can. It can get us dancing to its beat. But the power of music goes much, much further. Indeed, music occupies more areas of our brain than language does – humans are a musical species.

Obviously, for me and my colleagues and peers, the key in that quote is 'persuade us to buy something'. And while I can't point to a single, unifying theory that music can make a customer purchase certain products, there are some interesting studies which support the effect that music has on the shopping environment. We will cover those shortly.

MUSIC CAN BE THE MESSAGE

Some brands use music as a foreground component of their brand – becoming a tastemaker, being known for their music taste and style.

These brands encourage their audiences to discover new music and share what they have found, creating a conversation among their shoppers.

To illustrate this, I would like you to go to Twitter right now and hit the search bar. Type in the term 'playing' along with any tastemaker brand (think Urban Outfitter, Abercrombie & Fitch, American Apparel). You are guaranteed to see chatter among the audience – either loving (or hating) the music playing in these stores. In fact, at work, we use this all the time to measure how our soundtracks are doing among our clients' customers. It helps validate what we have promised for our clients – a compelling and engaging music soundtrack. Consumers who are tweeting the music heard in a store are engaged, whether it is intentional or not.

Even though we know that customers are avoiding advertising, we still see that consumers are moved by the music they heard during a 30- or 60-second spot. All over the web, there are websites dedicated to uncovering songs heard in a commercial (see adtunes.com, splendAd.com, for example). These consumers are having a conversation without the brand's involvement, which can be a good thing when people are eager to know the song they just heard. It continues to confound those of us experts in this field, however, why and how brands and the music industry have left it up to consumers to dig up this information on their own. That people are willing to build websites and share this information without anyone asking them to shows how overly compelling music is. Imagine how that conversation among consumers could go if it was actually facilitated by the brands themselves.

I first noticed this trend when I was working with AMC Network in 2007 to support their launch of the Emmy and Golden Globe-winning original series, *Mad Men*. I helped supervise the music for the network's rebranding campaign ('The Future of Classic'), which involved licensing music for more than 100 individual TV promo spots. We extended the music use for each promo beyond the spot and onto the AMC website, offering downloads, bios and photos of the artists featured. We focused on emerging artists and found that the bands were getting lots of new fans. Viewers of those spots went out of their way to seek out these artists, creating an engaging discovery component within the AMC and *Mad Men* brand experience. One artist even emailed me to tell me that their fan base had skyrocketed since the promotion. The client was very pleased with the campaign and later asked me in to host a conference with all their network partners (AMC, IFC, WE and Sundance), to educate marketing teams on how they can use music effectively when communicating with their customers.

Brands instinctively know that music is a powerful way to engage their audience. This use of music includes online website soundtracks, brand-promoted live events, artist partnerships or sponsorship relationships, content offerings (compilation CDs, free downloads, and, increasingly, free streams à la Spotify or Pandora), or by simply placing chyrons on ads.

When I left advertising in the early 2000s, I enrolled in NYU's Film Composition program while working at a prominent stock and original music house in New York City called DeWolfe Music. At DeWolfe, my clients included some of the world's biggest ad agencies (Saatchi & Saatchi, McCann Erickson, BBDO, Euro RSCG) and I helped guide the company to success, overseeing music, sales and content efforts. During this time, I began to fully understand the actual emotional and physiological reactions that music would have on a listener, and later I found studies that showed an actual relationship between music and consumer behavior or perception.

One of those, a 2000 study by Hargreaves, North and McKendrick[7] found that 'Music affects customers' estimates of the maximum sum they would pay for products.' Knowing that the right music compels an audience to increase the value of a product in their minds is extremely powerful. This goes back to our reason for collaborating to bring you this book in the first place – bringing value, adding value, using music to increase value to a brand.

Looking at restaurants, we have seen studies in which up-tempo music played, say, during lunch service would increase sales, or that diners stay longer and dine longer when slow-tempo music was played at night. This is something that restaurateurs already know – it is obvious – but the research underlines it.

Two studies in the late 1990s showed that music in a store is not a passive experience. The Gallup Organization Survey of 1996[8] found that '33% of shoppers admitted that the music in a store influenced their decision to make a purchase', while Music Choice reported in 1996[9] that '91% of shoppers said music affected their behavior'. Now, it may have affected them to leave the store or shop after a longer or shorter time, whatever, but it did affect them nonetheless. Music is clearly having an effect on your customers – so how can you harness that?

Today, there are countless ways that music can be a tool of engagement for brands. Free MP3s, tour sponsorships and remix contests are all ways of engaging with an audience, giving them something unique that they cannot get anywhere else. We follow this introduction with conversations with some of my actual clients about how a brand can use music to engage their customers. Some take a forward-thinking approach, while others try a more conventional route; some feel music is a cornerstone, while others view it as 'filling up the silence' in their stores. Either way, they all agree: the right music for the right customer experience is vital. Have you ever walked out of a store or restaurant because the music is so inappropriate or off in some way? If you answered yes, then you are halfway to understanding this power. In each case study that follows in Chapter 6, I will describe the process by which we created a brand-led custom music program. We did this using my methodology of creating an audio identity, which defines the brand, identifies the customers and bridges the two with music content.

Chapter 6

CASE STUDIES FOR MUSIC AS ENGAGEMENT

BY RICHARD JANKOVICH

BEAUTY AND THE BEAT: THE SOUND OF SEPHORA

LOOK GOOD, SOUND GOOD

THE $170 BILLION US COSMETICS industry is a fiercely competitive space with a variety of major players representing brands, distributors and retailers. In the early 2010s, this perpetually evolving industry was faced with the same recession-era worries that the entire retail economy was saddled with. However, women (not surprisingly the primary target for cosmetics) continued to value cosmetics, even in a down economy. Looking good, after all, results in feeling good and cosmetics represent a vital component of that process. The challenge for anyone in this space was attracting those paying customers as they tightened their belts, while continuing to appeal to their sense of beauty and confidence.

In early 2011, the national cosmetics retailer, Sephora, wanted to discuss some changes to their existing music program provided by Mood Media. Sephora was adjusting its entire retail strategy and its revitalized in-store experience needed to be supported by a consistent, strategic retail soundtrack. Originally launched in France, Sephora had been in the US market since 1998 and had quickly grown to be a formidable retailer with estimated revenue surpassing $1 billion from 750 store locations across 17 different countries.

'The music soundtrack is imperative to our retail experience,' said Liz Green, Sephora's Store Marketing Manager. 'It has the power to convey our brand's DNA and engage a client at the same time.' Liz was my day-to-day client contact at Sephora and as we began to examine the brand's soundtrack she played a key part in its direction. Sephora truly does value music and this is apparent in the amount of care it takes on a continuing basis to keep the program in line with its goals and vision. This approach is vital for success, as many clients still leave music decisions to the 11th hour and base these decisions primarily on their own subjective opinions or, worse, whatever is playing on their kids' iPods. As we continue to tell you, having a strategic commitment to and understanding of music, as a brand such as Sephora does, makes our jobs much easier in delivering a compelling and successful soundtrack and, of course, in delivering value through that soundtrack.

Sephora was and remains a unique client because its musical point of view is so strong. This is partly due to the fact that the brand had retained the veteran music producer, A&R scout and Red Hot Organization producer Paul Heck in order to help shape the vision. 'They were looking for a third party expert opinion on their music,' said Heck, when in 2010, uncertain of how to move forward with its music strategy, Sephora reached out to him to request some assistance. 'I tried to look at it simply, as an extra set of ears,' he explained. He spent time listening at various locations and forming a perspective on what was and wasn't working. One key component of Heck's recommendation was advising that Sephora stay away from the harsher elements of current pop music, as 'the music should never overwhelm the in-store experience'. He presented his concept to Sephora founded around simple directives: friendly, flowing, upbeat and uplifting. He included a starter playlist of music that would resonate with the brand's ideals and this feedback helped form the foundation for what the Sephora soundtrack would become. His 'Sephora Sound' creative brief became shorthand for Sephora's new soundtrack.

BUILDING A SOUND

'It's important for us to always select songs that reflect our brand essence,' explained Green when discussing Sephora's launch of a refresh of their brand. The existing tag line, 'The Beauty Authority', was being changed into something that reflected a more inspiring, creative and innovative message – 'Transforming Beauty'. When Sephora launched this new positioning, it was challenged by its CEO David Suliteanu to capture this campaign through a new, revived soundtrack. In fact, it was Suliteanu who suggested approaching a third party expert, which led to Heck's evaluation of the music. Sephora's new brand positioning was designed to be indicative of a more active and social relationship with its customers. 'Sephora Sound was designed to mirror that promise,' said Green. From where I sat I was convinced that a fresh new music soundtrack was the key component in delivering the right customer experience.

When Liz shared Heck's brief as well as the news of a brand refresh, I recognized there was a solid foundation from which to grow but felt I needed to learn much more. I suggested a content-geared, brand discovery workshop in order to feel our way through the brief, find the guardrails in which we would curate and, in general, better understand Sephora's entire retail strategy. In early 2011,

Liz and I got together with her programmers and account managers from Mood Media and dug in. In preparation for our meeting, I designed a discovery workshop which would take Liz through a series of discussions around her brand and her customers. My discovery workshops tend to avoid outright music discussion in order to keep us focused on goals and strategy. It is easy for clients and ourselves to get stuck in the rabbit-hole of subjective music opinion and I believe that before we can recommend a single song, we have a great deal of homework to do first.

In our workshop, I learned that in order to help Sephora with its new brand message, we needed to create common language and truly be able to articulate what it means to be 'Sephora'. I offered Liz a variety of exercises around the brand, in particular aimed at understanding their newly launched positioning of 'Transforming Beauty'. I conducted a variety of keyword discussions, comparisons of emotional/personality traits, celebrity representations and other icons that allow us to better understand any dimension of a brand. Those with a background in branding will find these types of exercises very familiar. I facilitated exercises around the Sephora customer that helped us understand exactly what they were looking for from the brand. One key learning point from this customer exercise is that their customers are open to new things and we knew we could reflect that through music. I learned that the Sephora brand was centered on being inspiring, creative and innovative while offering broad, unique selections, fun interactive experiences and unbiased personalized services. The challenge was to create a music program that articulated all elements of the brand while delivering something that would resonate with customers. Overall, the discovery session yielded the information we needed.

Right away, I looked for some low-hanging fruit that could immediately impact the program. We wanted to increase the size of the program by 250 songs to accommodate the desire for a more eclectic offering, as well as assuage fears that repeat customers were becoming burned out with the soundtrack. This was accomplished through a combination of searching from our licensed pool of music as well as reaching out to many contacts in the music industry for new tracks that were yet to hit the market. My friends at record labels and music publishers were frantically forwarding me MP3s while jumping from club to club as it happened to be the middle of SXSW, the year's biggest music conference held in Austin, Texas.

I designed the new program for Sephora so that it would truly make the brand 'pop' in this competitive retail landscape, and the program was quickly approved. The overall make-up of this soundtrack is a unique one indeed. Customers hear light doses of critically acclaimed pop hits by Robyn, Swedish House Mafia and Coldplay alongside the best emerging tracks by rising indie pop acts like Broken Bells, The Naked and Famous and The xx. Additionally, imagine your older sibling's favorite classics by credible innovators like The Smiths, Roxy Music and Elastica complementing a collection of forward-looking electro-pop tracks by Tanlines, Austra and Toro y Moi. If you are unfamiliar with these artists, a quick Google search should yield music samples or YouTube clips. These various styles, all aligned around the Sephora brand, come together to create an experience at once both comforting and exciting. This allows Sephora's customers to bob their head while they shop and make mental notes of fresh new tracks to add to their Spotify playlists at home.

THE FLOW OF ENERGY

Additionally, we pursued a strategy around 'day-parting'. Day-parting refers to building subsets of a brand's retail soundtrack designed to play during specific times of the day. So, for instance, if your morning crowd skews in any demographic direction – older, younger, more male, more female – you can craft playlists from your main brand soundtrack that might be more appropriate for them.

Typically, day-parting is used to accommodate different energy levels. No one expects to hear raucous, thumping music at eight o'clock in the morning when the doors open. In Sephora's case, we designed day-parting to help create a flow of energy depending on the time of day. For instance, from opening to lunch, the soundtrack is mellower than usual, careful to avoid anything frenetic, while the five o'clock-to-close soundtrack is considerably more upbeat, playing to that after-work crowd or those stopping in on their way out for a night on the town.

One challenge with the morning soundtrack is to still maintain a level of positivity. 'How can you be mellow without being depressing?' asked Green. We accomplished this through a careful, hand-picked selection of songs that are still core to the brand's attributes but presented in a more relaxed manner. This is determined by looking at a song's tempo and time signature, timbre of instrumentation, density of sound, lyrical content and more. These criteria are not hard-and-fast rules – it all requires the skilled touch of a music branding expert or veteran music programmer. For example, 'Friday I'm In Love' by The Cure has an upbeat, speedy rhythm, but the combination of light acoustic guitar, chirping piano melodies and playful, soft delivery by vocalist Robert Smith amounts to a perfect piece for the morning chill crowd. In stark contrast, Kimbra's 'Settle Down' is an infectious piece surrounded by sparse instrumentation and a lower than usual tempo built around a unique drumbeat. What both of these songs share in common is that sense of discovery and uniqueness at the core of the Sephora brand experience. The diversity between these two pieces in and of itself is a reflection of the brand. 'Not every song should sound the same,' Green continued. 'We strive for an eclectic and diverse sound balancing what's new and hot right now, breaking it up with older classics.'

When Sephora first launched in the United States in 1998, it was, of course, new and unfamiliar to the market. The retailer's ethos was to introduce the US market to new, up-and-coming cosmetic brands. These untested brands were nurtured within Sephora's environment and given the ability to grow and succeed. 'In the beginning, we acted like a boutique focused on grass-roots brands that needed a place to sell their product,' says Green. This dedication to exposing their audience to new, indie products is reflected in the soundtrack. 'We want our customers to find new products and new music that they can take with them in their lives,' says Green. 'This affords us the ability to help new artists to reach ears that wouldn't normally have heard their songs.'

TESTING FOR SUCCESS

Sephora knows its music soundtrack choices have been a success. Like most brands, it regularly conducts market research to ensure it is delivering on its brand promise to its customers. In many surveys, Sephora can isolate the raw data to see what its clients are saying about the music. In fact, this was part of the reason for the initial refinement. Sephora had found feedback related to the music that we were able to address. Today the Sephora Sound program has been met with enthusiasm by their customers.

'People ask us a lot…what is playing,' Green explained. Every month, Sephora gets emails from customers eager to help them identify a particular song and customers routinely ask the store associates to find out the name of a song that is playing. Green explains that their customers take note of what is playing because 'music is important in their life and the right mix fosters a positive shopping experience'. Regularly seeing these customers sing or dance along is the best reward and a sign that we were doing the right thing. 'We want our clients to embrace Sephora Sound and foster a passage of returning enjoyment and discovery,' continued Green.

In addition, Sephora avidly tracks their clients' social media chatter and have found that the music playing in their stores is an often-referenced topic of Facebook and Twitter comments. In fact, since Sephora first suggested it to me, I now make it a point to track social media chatter whenever we launch a new soundtrack for a brand. There is nothing more gratifying than an 'OMG! Can't believe I just heard my favorite song playing at...' tweet to make us realize that we are delivering on our promise to clients.

Beyond their customer base, Sephora's in-store staff were another consideration. Store associates, regardless of the retailer for whom they work, can often be negatively affected by repetition and may have strong opinions about the music that accompanies them on their shift. 'Our associates always prefer poppy music that they are hearing on the radio,' said Green. However, what Sephora found was that its eclectic program balancing pop music with emerging, under-ground and edgier styles was really engaging with their employees. 'They often run back to the player to see what's playing and making a note of it,' said Green. 'It is great that we are exposing our cast members to new songs that they might not have otherwise heard.'

BEYOND RETAIL

Beyond the retail soundtrack, Sephora considers music to be a strong asset to its brand. It often features in-store events with DJs and it needed to ensure that its new audio identity was still being adhered to. 'We give our DJs the same guidelines we established when we launched the new soundtrack,' said Green. The DJs are able to add their own spin to it and work at keeping the mood more upbeat, but they understand the brand's audio guidelines to deliver a consistent and intentional soundtrack. We find that they often use the same songs from the retail soundtrack, something I recommend to many clients, and I have seen my audio identities passed around from brand to agency to DJ and back again.

In late 2011, Sephora was launching a new iPad app that would feature different looks (Bold Glamour or Unexpected Edge, for instance) for its customers to engage with its products. Again, Sephora looked to us to identify and license appropriate music that reinforced the brand, while fulfilling the immediate tactical needs of the iPad app. As the guardians of Sephora's audio identity, we scoured the world of music for the right acts and negotiated the license to include their songs. This provided an added benefit in that we could also license these same songs for use in the in-store playlist, creating a 360-degree approach to music and branding.

'Last year, we did Fridays at the Beauty Studio,' said Green. At its Fifth Avenue flagship location in Manhattan, Sephora again worked with Paul Heck to deliver on a series of live music events centered on featured cosmetics brands. This resulted in some memorable performances by a variety of artists, including the high-energy dance of Jessica Six, the thoughtful indie folk of Nicole Atkins and the retro-soul/funk of Quadron. Each artist was given direction on what Sephora was looking for and the artists were happy to oblige, playing 45-minute sets that they vigorously promoted on their own websites and social media channels. This led to lots of the bands' fans coming to Sephora, many of whom would not ordinarily have visited the retailer. Some of these events were even covered on music blogs.

KEEPING ON TRACK

To ensure the Sephora Sound program remains on target, once a month Liz previews the current selections. As well as adding new songs, programmers also remove (or 'rest') other songs that may have become played out either in the soundtrack or in popular culture. Liz works closely with the programming team providing direct feedback on each song, which helps with future selections, and she often provides a list of new music she has sourced herself – often found on blogs – which gets acquired and licensed for her. In fact, Liz reminded me that I utilized my own personal connections in order to license OK Go's 'White Knuckles' for her program. The licensing conversations had stalled until I recalled that I knew their manager and took a pro-active approach to getting the song cleared for use. It was a win–win for both the band and Sephora.

When deciding on music selections, Green says she is always thinking about her clients first, imagining that she is in a store and putting herself in the shoes of everyone from an 8-year old girl to a 70-year-old woman. The Sephora customer is a healthy cross-section of the female population and represents people from all walks of life. With a large demographic to consider, many brands will opt for a 'one size fits all' soundtrack – something that is designed not to offend anyone. This often results in a homogenous and worn-out playlist of safe hit songs from the pop music canon that inevitably mirrors countless radio stations, TV ads, film soundtracks and hundreds of other retail soundtracks delivering a forgettable, brand-agnostic experience. Not so with Sephora. 'We do have a wide range of demographics and we can't risk alienating them,' said Green, 'so the challenge becomes appealing to these customers without being generic.' Sephora established a vision around its brand and its soundtrack matched that. It was a bold move and one that makes the brand memorable to its clients. 'We were looking to create something that sounds different from other retailers,' says Green.

When asked if Sephora was considered a tastemaker in music, Green smiled and said 'We hope so!' She went on to explain that Sephora wants its customers to pay attention and notice the music that is playing. 'We want to be seen as experts in everything we do; if you can discover a new band or song while you're picking up your lip-gloss, that's fantastic!'

SMASHING CONVENTIONS: THE SMASHBURGER SOUNDTRACK

HUNGRY FOR MUSIC

It's not every day that a well-established business vertical such as 'burger joints' gets revolutionized and challenged by a young upstart. The fast food burger empires simply had no idea that Denver's scrappy Smashburger would not only nip at their heels but also grow into a formidable competitor. Launched in 2007, Smashburger has grown quickly to 150 locations in just a few short years and was named 'America's Most Promising Company' by *Forbes* magazine in 2011.

Named after its cooking process (literally smashing the burger on the grill to lock in the juices), Smashburger is a leader in the relatively new vertical called 'Fast Casual' (see also Chipotle, Panera and Così). This differentiates itself by offering a more enjoyable dining experience, fresher ingredients, more eclectic menu offerings and even a beer and wine list. Fast Casual restaurants offer the same convenience and relative speed one expects from a typical quick service restaurant or fast food spot, but with fare that is more unusual and often includes an intentionally engaging customer experience.

What major fast food marketers miss is exactly what a company like Smashburger provides – a new take on an old idea. Part of that new idea involves music and when Smashburger was ready to create a branded music concept, I helped their growing brand stand out in this crowded field. I have had the pleasure of working with Smashbuger over the past few years, creating a soundtrack of music that would appeal to their target demographic and accentuate the uniqueness of their business.

Every year the average American eats 43 hamburgers, and Tom Ryan, founder of Smashburger, is intent on those being his burgers. He was kind enough to spend some time with me, discussing the importance of music to the Smashburger brand. While we had worked directly with his branding and marketing team, Tom was clearly the visionary behind the brand. He told me that he believes all modern brands are defined by what they put in front of their customers. This includes all the elements of the customer experience and how those stimuli can engage with customers' senses, hearts and minds. Smashburger's competitive landscape is massive. It is so broad, in fact, that it becomes a challenge to do direct comparisons when evaluating the brand. And yet within this large scale, it finds that music is key to helping it to be different. Smashburger's goal was to be, in Ryan's words, 'modern, differentiated, added value' by using its assets beyond food: ambience, decor, music and more.

'Being a restaurant,' Ryan said, 'we know that some senses are more important than others.' The smell of food, for instance, is a key component of any restaurant, but it is the entire experience coming together which differentiates Smashburger in the marketplace – the decor, the color scheme, the flow of the customer experience and, of course, the nascent and directed sound of the restaurant.

Smashburger's initial music soundtrack was built around the brand's marketing keywords of 'Smash, Sizzle, Savor'. It was a simple system of rationalizing music that was delivered via a talented programming team and vast technology infrastructure. In 2011 Smashburger was growing at an impressive clip, so they asked for a true experience design that would provide direction for all in-location media and content (music, visuals, sound and so on). The brief for Smashburger was clear – they were moving away from 'Smash, Sizzle, Savor' toward a new positioning of 'Smashed Fresh. Served Delicious.' The music soundtrack needed to bring this new idea to life. In doing so it would reinforce that smashing is better, that their product could be customized, that their ingredients were fresh and that their award-winning extensive menu was still a local place open to all. Specifically, we were going to have to improve store energy and bring to life their brand personality, satisfying guests as they dined in this modern, high-energy space.

DIG IN

We hosted the brand for a day-long workshop, along with a series of events. We wanted the day to be memorable beyond the brand discovery work so we scheduled a live performance by an up-and-coming band and hosted an outside barbecue party featuring Smashburger fare. Many attended, ate some burgers and soaked up the sounds of A Rocket To The Moon, who were at the time on tour, opening for The All-American Rejects. After the live performance, the client entered a conference room accompanied by the soaring chorus of 'Smash It Up' by The Damned.

Any skyrocketing young brand faces challenges and this team was well aware of the need for an articulated brand experience to preserve its uniqueness as it grew. Its coherent brand identity was dissected to reveal what makes Smashburger unique and full of charm. I crafted our workshop around this framework, hoping to address its needs while bringing additional meaning to its brand.

One of the first exercises we did was around brand personality traits. The client had provided us with some brand personality traits and we asked them to rank them in order of priority to the brand. This short list of brand traits would later drive a great deal of the media strategy for the in-restaurant music and is an exercise we undertake with many of our brand partners – just as we did with Sephora and Sunglass Hut mentioned elsewhere in this chapter. Clients often hire branding firms to come up with these words and sometimes the words need further clarification. For instance, a telecommunications brand might consider itself 'welcoming'. But 'welcoming' might mean nurturing, motherly embraces to one person while the brand had intended it to mean helpful and service-oriented. So we parse these words by giving our clients options to illustrate what they mean. For example, for 'welcoming' we might give them a series of photos – a family physician, a teacher, an open door – and ask them to choose which is closest to their intent.

Beyond the components of the brand itself, Smashburger had identified a handful of customer archetypes based on the demographic information of their guests. These archetypes helped us really understand how to use music content to reach out and communicate the brand's personality. For instance, one customer archetype may have an affinity for mass-marketed music, which is known from market research. That doesn't necessarily mean I would program it to be exclusively Top 40, but it could color how to paint the brand through music. If the brand is interested in challenging these clients, we might look slightly left of the mainstream – not quite to the outer reaches of, say, Spacemen 3 or Sonic Youth, but just slightly out of the mass-market to artists like Lenka or Foster the People. This type of nuance is what we explored in our session with Smashburger. They knew their archetypes but we needed to know more – the television programs they watch, the books they read, where they shop, the cars they drive.

Each Smashburger archetype was profiled in a way that added meaning to the types of people they are and the lives they lead. They had presented us with 14 distinct customer archetypes based on income level, geography, lifestyle, aspirations and education. Of those 14 archetypes, we wanted to find common threads that could help drive a unified music experience. We narrowed down some common themes related to how they consume music and culture. For their more adventurous archetypes, we needed to explore just how willing they were to explore their own eclecticism. Were they more likely to drink wine at a wine tasting or grow their own organic vegetables? Were they more likely to read *Dwell* or *Vanity Fair*? Would they take a walking tour of Paris or relax on a Caribbean cruise? Once we get the room to show consensus, we begin to see patterns emerge and these patterns allow us to truly know the audience to whom we are programming. We also learned the average dining experience lasts 25 minutes, which impacted how we program songs to play via our scheduling software. Everything we learned from the workshop resulted in a fresh audio identity, which drove the programming in the restaurants. Beyond the type of music we chose, we always enforced strict rules about content appropriateness. For Smashburger, we needed to appeal to a family audience and made sure to avoid any heavy or dark themes, always keeping an emphasis on approachability. This, in addition to stringent lyrical standards, would ensure that even as we engaged our audience, we would never alienate or offend their sensibilities.

FOREVER 32

The customer archetypes we reviewed were all grounded within Ryan's vision for his audience: 'We thought very hard during the early stages of brand development about what kind of music would support and reach the target audience.' One way to define the brand's sound was to focus on its target audience and move backwards from there. 'It becomes an interesting question for us,' continues Ryan. 'When burgers are such a universal American favorite food, who is your target?'

For Smashburger, what drives the decor and sensory experience is the desire to engage with this massive demographic target. 'How do I want to make people feel regardless of who they are?' asks Ryan. As a brand that defies conventional customer targets, they needed to find something unifying that would extend to these various personality, age, income and geographic distinctions. Ryan and his team ultimately settled on the age of 32.

'There is something magical about the age of 32,' says Ryan. He explained that 32-year-olds are at a perfect point in their life development – young enough to be social and exploring new things, while theoretically being old enough to actually afford that lifestyle. Beyond that, he feels that it is an aspirational age. He theorizes that those under 32 yearn to reach that age as they expect their careers and adult lives to be in full swing by then while those over 32 remember that age fondly, trying to hold onto that frame of mind. We jokingly referred to it as 'Forever 32'. The 32-year-old lifestyle and its relationship to pop culture and contemporary styles supersede the elements of mass-market life. By targeting here, Smashburger is able to create an aspirational experience while also engaging those in that core target.

'As we thought about music, I knew we needed something that was on target for a cool 32-year-old,' said Ryan. This is the benchmark that Smashburger uses to measure success and we ensured that the music program provides just that. This extends beyond music selection into sound systems. Not only did we craft a custom music program but we deliver it over top-of-the-range sound systems as we know those 'cool 32-year-olds' are focused on sound quality and have the funds to acquire high-end music systems at home. Concentrating on the 32-year-old ensures that the brand will always be modern. After all, each year the 32-year-old archetype changes according to current art, culture and food trends and tastes.

For 32-year-olds in 2012, we looked to a uniquely expressive playlist that avoids bubblegum and overtly electronic styles, looking at emerging domestic and international trends while still being rooted in contemporary pop structures. A track like 'Janglin'' by Edward Sharpe and the Magnetic Zeros represents a style of independent music-making which happens to cross over into mainstream earbuds. The instantly memorable vocal line of 'ooh ah, Ooh ah, bah bah dah bah dah bah' atop a bouncy beat and acoustic interplay was the centerpiece for a Ford Fiesta campaign in 2010. The song itself is a pleasant slice of both 60s psych pop with a dash of *Joseph and the Technicolor Dreamcoat* theatricality, but still manages to remain firmly rooted in the modern Los Angeles indie scene. Add to all that the larger-than-life character of lead singer Alex Ebert (who also fronted the avant-garde indie rock band Ima Robot) and you have a truly unforgettable pop song. 'Janglin'' and its ilk were not billboard charting songs or artists but they had achieved some familiarity through their prevalence in commercials, television shows, movies and even video game soundtracks. And while this style does bring an alternative approach to the mainstream, the formats and song structures remain consistent with popular music forms, such as verses, choruses and the occasional hook.

Conversely, our 32-year-olds also resonate with older songs that have retained their edginess over the years. For instance, 'Two Hearts Beat As One' by U2 is the perfect slice of 80s college rock that is immediately hummable and approachable, even by those who have only a cursory knowledge of the track. The track is packed with everything we expect from vintage U2 – a frantic guitar riff by The Edge, soaring Bono vocals, steady rhythm, authentic passion and post-punk/new wave nuances. But given its place as the *other* single from U2's 1983 breakout album *War* (neither 'Sunday Bloody Sunday' nor 'New Year's Day'), the song feels fresh and stimulating to today's ears. Even the subject matter of 'Two Hearts Beat As One' seems perfect for Smashburger – it is an ode to finding harmony and love and is often considered a love song from Bono to his mother. A collection of similar 'cool classics' mixes in with the cross-over indie mentioned above, as well as hundreds of other songs in the Smashburger program to deliver a captivating listen to this unique restaurant experience.

INNOVATING WHILE ENGAGING

Smashburger has also taken an innovative approach to its employees, incentivizing efficiency and building fans out of their workers. During my conversation with Ryan, I asked about the effect on his employees' mood, because they have to listen every day, all day to the song choices. Ryan indicated that the employees grasp the importance of a branded soundtrack and that most of the time they agree that it is the right blend of songs. What is even more interesting to Ryan is that his team feels involved in the musical discovery. Employees are often downloading songs for themselves or checking what is playing on the system.

As the brand has extended its footprint out of the United States and into other areas, music has been key. In Kuwait, the employees are very interested in the Western-influenced soundtrack. They want to stream the music to their website and help bring these fascinating sounds to the Kuwaiti audience. The employees as well as the customers are absorbing the soundtrack with a lot of energy and fanfare, leading Ryan to recognize that music is a powerful component of this global brand. 'The more the music sticks out relative to differentiation, the more it provides customers with energy and discovery,' said Ryan. Though the strategy and design remain the same, the actual songs in the overseas program veer from the American playlist in order to appeal to a different audience with radically different touchpoints with American culture.

And just how does Smashburger know that the music is hitting the mark? 'When people are in the restaurant, holding up their iPhones to identify a song or asking our team what song is playing,' said Ryan, 'then you know we have just added value to the marketplace.' The music is not going to be noticed by everybody, however, as for many it just fades into the background. But during key moments of the day, when diners tend to linger (say, around 3 pm or the post-date, late-night crowd), Smashburger notices more and more people listening to the music and taking note of the songs that are playing. 'People are hanging out, doing homework and they tend to listen more deeply,' added Ryan.

CREATIVE EXPRESSIONS

In Ryan's view, there is a link between music and food. 'They have a lot of similarities as there are countless numbers of creative expressions around both – how many cool recipes or new albums still come out every year?' It is an interesting point. These two passions and art forms continue to reinvent themselves, year after year, whether it's through an entirely new idea, fusing existing styles or revisiting prior concepts.

Beyond the restaurant soundtrack itself, music has been a major component of the Smashburger brand experience since the beginning. During openings of some of the earliest restaurants, they would engage with the local music community in a grass-roots way, involving them through events and contests. For instance, a local band could enter a contest to win a slot at an opening event. Scores of local bands and artists would sign up and encourage their fans to vote for them on the Smashburger website. The band with the most votes would win the headlining slot, playing to all the opening-day customers. This was an ingenious way of engaging with the local music community by offering them an opportunity, as well as harnessing the power of their individual fan bases when each bands' following showed up at this new burger restaurant. 'I remembered telling my staff I wanted the audio equivalent of a spotlight to draw people in,' said Ryan, 'and these bands performing would attract curious passers-by.'

The brand continues to use music in its internal messaging and web videos and can also see how music can be expanded as the brand grows. 'I could see us having a web-streaming solution or something that could live on social media,' says Ryan. For now, having a credible, articulated audio identity is an important piece of the puzzle. As this young brand grows, we will be there helping to oversee its music choices and delivering an engaging customer experience.

I GOTTA WEAR SHADES: SUNGLASS HUT'S MUSIC PROGRAM

THE FUTURE'S SO BRIGHT

From its humble beginnings in 1971 as a single kiosk in a Florida mall, to a premier brand within the publicly traded Luxottica family,

Sunglass Hut is now the leading retailer for fashion and style sunglasses. Such organic growth is exciting but comes with a unique set of challenges, not the least of which is maintaining a consistent brand and customer experience. Brands that grow slowly must keep a watchful eye to ensure that their original ethos can evolve with the growth trajectory. Otherwise, they can find themselves in a situation where what once made the brand special and unique is no longer resonating with the public.

With about 3300 locations worldwide, Sunglass Hut is no stranger to retail operations, and they have placed a great deal of emphasis and value in transforming their stores into engaging and innovative spaces for their customers. In addition to store fixtures, lighting, staff and signage, the brand fully believes in the importance of a strategic music experience as key to maintaining the original value and ethos of the brand. With locations all over the globe, Sunglass Hut needed me to craft a single, cohesive music program for the US, Canadian and Puerto Rican markets. I did so using strategic reasoning.

'Music is a critical aspect of the overall store experience,' says Jeff Fisher, Senior Director of Store Experience. Along with Sara Sullivan, Senior Manager of Store Experience, Fisher and the Sunglass Hut brand truly walk the walk when it comes to their trumpeting of music's value, investing in multi-day music brand conferences, internal adoption tools and a robust, complex music program. 'Music is especially important for us as a leading fashion brand,' says Fisher. Music and fashion have an inextricable link going back to the origins of each. Consider examples as varied as designer Coco Chanel and composer Igor Stravinsky's partnership, model Nico and the psychedelic pop group The Velvet Underground's music–fashion blended career, or more recently Justin Timberlake's William Rast denim line, Gwen Stefani's L.A.M.B. clothing products or simply Lady Gaga's undeniable influence on fashion trends.

In our society we often ascribe meaning to the music we listen to. A 2008 study by Professors Adrian North and Daniel Hargreaves[1] showed that music can be an indicator of your personality type. The study surveyed 36,000 music listeners in over 60 countries and asked them to describe their personality and indicate their preferred music genres. The research found that heavy metal listeners are creative but shy, and indie music listeners had low self-esteem. Country music fans are hard-working, while hip-hop listeners are outgoing. These very same attributes can be detected by consumers and applied to a brand, which is why we believe that strategic music selection is so important.

TRANSFORMATIONAL THINGS

'Overall, we have fun music which aligns with our product,' says Fisher. Their music program is at its foundation fun and upbeat, replicating a party atmosphere to create a high-energy retail space. This is particularly important in smaller stores where only a single associate may be working. 'People beget more people,' says Fisher. 'Music brings them in, creating energy where it might have been lacking before.' And music not only improves energy levels but also affects the attitude of the consumer. 'Both sunglasses and music make you feel good,' adds Sullivan, 'and we believe you never have a bad day wearing sunglasses.'

'I really think that sunglasses themselves are transformative things.' says Fisher, 'People like to play and try on different styles and they are willing to explore their personality through sunglasses. Whether it's Schwarzenegger donning shades as the Terminator, Clint Eastwood's Dirty Harry specs, Corey Hart's ode to wearing 'Sunglasses At Night' or Bob Dylan's ever-present Wayfarers, this iconic power leads consumers to inhabit these personae by the very act of playing with Sunglass Hut's products. To foster this type of playful environment, Sunglass Hut doesn't keep its products under glass – they are accessible to anyone in the store and consumers are encouraged to try them on. 'The music helps underscore this hands-on experience,' says Fisher, 'and you see people willing to play with the product while clearly enjoying the music, dancing along.'

Sullivan explains that music is important, not just inside each location but also as a magnet to attract passers-by. 'We invest a lot in order to project our stores outward,' adds Sullivan, 'and music is a key part of that strategy.' Sunglass Hut has some of their own research that supports this. For instance, when stores are playing music near the entrance they draw in more consumers and as a result have higher sales. 'We've looked at stores with music versus stores without,' continues Sullivan, 'and nine times out of ten the results are stronger in stores where music helps draw the consumer in.' Additionally, Sunglass Hut has seen that without music, its business actually suffers. 'There was one store where the music went out and they missed their sales goals – this is how we know music is a huge asset for us,' explains Fisher.

Beyond the content itself, brands also have a variety of choices to make when they determine how to physically place music in their stores. Speaker placement, wiring and zoning all come into play. Each area serviced by a set of speakers is considered a separate zone. Stores can have multiple zones playing the same or different content. For Sunglass Hut, each store has a uniquely customized acoustic design depending on size and location, among other factors. 'It depends on each store experience,' says Sullivan. 'We use music at the storefront to attract people but also at the cashwrap when people are paying for their purchases.' They elected to zone these areas differently to allow control over volume. Though the content is the same, the volume at the storefront is loud enough to draw people in while lower at the cashwrap, allowing for conversations at the till. Generally, stores have two zones with unique volume controls but flagships might have three or four. Sunglass Hut deliberately allows music to spill over the lease line attracting those elusive passers-by, and in general do not consider music to be 'ambience', but rather an active part of the experience. 'It's a key component,' says Fisher, 'like the materials, the layout, the product, the role of the associate, the transaction, the music – all these elements come together and are all equally important.'

NAVIGATING FEEDBACK FROM ALL AREAS

The engaging aspects of Sunglass Hut's music program are apparent with customers who are visibly interested in the content. 'Hands holding up iPhones with the Shazam app are pretty common in the stores,' says Sullivan. Their employees are always speaking to customers about the music, which keeps them engaged with the brand. 'We get good feedback on consumer interaction on what a song might be,' adds Sullivan. What's even better than customer delight in music is the lack of negative feedback. 'We haven't had a single complaint in nearly two years,' adds Sullivan. Choosing the right content for this program is where expertise really comes in. We apply our methodology of understanding the key components of the brand, uncovering the vital traits of each customer type and crafting a programming solution that completes the retail relationship between brand and consumer. And beyond customers, Fisher says it helps engage with the associates as well. 'It's not just for customers but is a key element that helps our associates maintain a level of energy, excitement and atmosphere,' says Fisher. Sunglass Hut has found that their employees are quite passionate about music in general. 'They love hearing new songs,' says Sullivan, 'and want to be inspired.' The new music in the program can make even their savviest employees turn their heads. 'We love to catch them off-guard,' admits Fisher.

Perhaps the most unique point of view from Sunglass Hut is the role of their associates. Many (actually most) brands I work with respect their associates' opinions on music, but tend to drive

top-down with a music vision. The heads of marketing or operations better understand the corporate vision and we work diligently
to provide that in a way that engages with their staff, as much as
their customers. But Sunglass Hut had a different take. 'Our associates live and breathe the brand every day,' says Fisher, 'they get lots of
feedback from consumers.' Sunglass Hut believes that these associates, being both the constant daily representation of their brand as
well as a resource for customer market research, should be deeply
involved in how the brand enhances and refines the retail experience. 'We thought "Why don't we assemble a panel of associates who
understand who we are as a brand and can help influence the music
we put out every day?"' says Sullivan. In 2011, Sunglass Hut created
their first Music Board. This initial iteration included staff from all
over their footprint and featured a variety of employees, from associates to store managers to regional trainers.

Prior to 2011, Sunglass Hut's music program was being refreshed
on a regular basis. When they came to me in early 2011 with their
idea for the Music Board, I listened intently. Never before had a client suggested such a broad group of stakeholders and I considered
this both a challenge but also an exciting opportunity. Sunglass Hut
began by sending a questionnaire to all their employees along with
an application to join the board. 'It was overwhelming,' explains
Sullivan, 'we had almost 300 applicants!' Not surprising, since everyone loves to talk about music. They selected two employees from
each region, collecting 18 personalities from all over the country.
The challenge, of course, would be to manage disparate points of
view, while fostering discussion and debate, on a subject as personal
as music. But the chance to dive into the brand, educate their stakeholders and really help them all engage with music more deeply was
exciting. We proposed a two-day event in which all members of the
Music Board would convene to learn about music branding, the
music industry, and branding in general.

CREATING AN AUDIO IDENTITY

In mid-2011, I hosted the first Sunglass Hut Music Summit and treated our client to workshops, lectures, panels and live music. In order to train our Music Board to think of music in brand terms, rather than personal taste, I designed a light introductory exercise to help individually engage with each member. Prior to the exercise, each member of the board provided us with a few bits of information about themselves: how they get to work, the last meal they ate, the last movie they saw, and so on. We used this limited information to create a profile for each of them, similar to profiles we create for customer archetypes or brand attributes. We then took our 18 profiles and assigned them to a music programmer to select three songs that represented each. We began our conference by bringing each Music Board member to the front of the room, walking through their profile, playing the three songs suggested by our programmer and letting the room decide which was most appropriate as their theme song. Not only was it very engaging and fun, but it really helped prepare them to approach music as an outsider. Letting their peers decide the right music to represent them, based on a limited amount of information, was the perfect primer for the rest of the conference. We even conducted the exercises on ourselves to join in the fun and act as an icebreaker. For instance, my profile indicated that I drive a Mini Cooper, shop at Zara, read *Paper* magazine and love Ethiopian food – all true. It was an unsettling but rewarding experience having a room of 25 strangers determine that 'Gamma Ray' by Beck was the perfect theme song for the archetype of 'Richard Jankovich'. The rest of the 2011 conference featured discussions of what branding really means, the history of music in brands, a discussion of the 'Sound Of Sunglass Hut', break-out sessions exploring how they could use music as a marketing tool and a live event in a local venue featuring a touring artist. All in all, our clients at Sunglass Hut were ecstatic with the event and they quickly booked a subsequent conference for early 2012.

With the involvement of the Music Board and a commitment to the importance of music, the only remaining challenge was to articulate how the music soundtrack would reflect the brand's values to the customer base. In order to develop an audio identity we analyzed Sunglass Hut's brand materials, the feedback from our conference, its customer demographic information, its history with music and how it presented itself to the public. This process involved interviews and meetings with Fisher, Sullivan and other members of the Sunglass Hut brand team. The exercise uncovered the brand's five main attributes that could be best expressed through music, and provided a programming strategy to reinforce each one. For instance, one brand trait is 'inspiring,' which we extracted from Sunglass Hut's desire to help customers realize their potential and the feeling of inspiration one gets from a pair of sunglasses. The brand already inspires its customers through fresh ideas and exciting retail presentation, harnessing creativity and originality to express aspirational style. Our challenge was to select a music concept that would complement the brand's efforts. We presented a collection of indie and emerging pop tracks that met the filters of 'striving' and 'stimulating' without taking themselves too seriously, or veering off into cliché notions of 'inspiration'. We looked to up-and-coming artists on the brink of stardom and placed them alongside forward-thinking indie pop and rock tracks, ensuring that all were grounded in common variables. These included progressive production, interesting song structures, occasional lo-fi tendencies and cutting-edge ideas around instrumentation, style and genre. Example songs from our 'inspiring' category included the challenging art-pop of Lykke Li's 'Youth Knows No Pain', the exciting synth-pop of 'True Love' from Friendly Fires and the adventurous psychedelic soul of Theophilus London's 'Wine and Chocolates'. Collectively, these songs represented music that would engage and excite customers in a way specific to Sunglass Hut's concept of 'inspiring'. Each of the other brand attributes had their own relevant concepts, which were also approved by Sunglass Hut. Together, they formed the basis for a targeted unique program and our audio identity was approved and implemented.

LAUNCHING AND MAINTAINING THE MUSIC PROGRAM

'Usually it's "here's your brand deck and here's some ideas", but the work that you guys did, diving into the brand in order to rationalize how music accentuates brand traits was impressive,' says Fisher. 'It was so thoroughly thought out and allowed for a framework that we can judge our music against.' The audio identity was rolled out to the Music Board during the 2012 conference and they embraced it as the tool with which they could evaluate music choices. 'During our monthly review, we literally refer back to it – does this song's identity align with this brand trait? Does it feel "inspiring"? Does it meet our criteria?' says Sullivan. All in all, it was a rare moment of true collaboration – one that has grown each month as we all continue to refine our approach. 'We've used the audio identity internally for other purposes,' admits Fisher. 'We've shared it with our peers within marketing and they've found it very helpful as well for selecting music for our videos, our events, our internal summit and annual conference.' This is the true value of having strategic guidelines for music selection – it allows a brand to rest easy knowing that a rationale exists for a historically subjective process.

The 2012 Music Board was refined to a smaller group and Sunglass Hut was very strategic in selecting each member. 'We really honed in on a brand-savvy group,' explains Fisher. This leaner group was trained to fully understand the criteria and our workshops really helped them align brand to music. In January 2012, we met the Music Board in New York City for a two-day intensive workshop; this included a discussion of their refined audio identity, a panel including music industry insiders and artists, and a live performance and meet-and-greet with an artist from the Sunglass Hut program.

With the audio identity approved and blessed by all members of the Music Board, we were able to build and launch their music program. For a client such as Sunglass Hut, I typically launch with a fully built program (generally in the range of 500 to 800 songs) that gets maintained on a certain rotation. With every rotation (monthly, bi-monthly or quarterly) a brand-savvy music programmer reviews the program, removes songs that have burned out, adds new songs that are appropriate for the brand and adjusts the playclock (the process which determines how often and which songs play during the day). With our Music Board's involvement, we needed to develop a tool to keep them engaged as the music soundtrack changes and evolves with every rotation. We could not rely on typical client communication tools such as instant messaging or email chains to facilitate a conversation, so we created Behind Dark Glasses, the internal employee music blog for Sunglass Hut. Each member of the board logs in to review new song additions to the program and offer their feedback, which can be shared and commented on by their peers. They can debate with each other (or with us) on our proposed additions or suggest new songs for the program. The blog even fosters a dialogue about music in general with members exchanging bands for each to check out. Using the blog, our team is able to evaluate the feedback, identify consensus and move ahead with each update to the program, thereby streamlining what could have become a difficult process. All the feedback from the blog directly informs and drives the actual music program which inspires the associates.

In 2013, I hosted the third annual Music and Branding Summit for Sunglass Hut. We spent a jam-packed, music-infused two days nestled in a tranquil space in the Silverlake neighborhood of Los Angeles. As in earlier years, I presented a 'Music and Branding' overview, excerpts from this book, and led a discussion of the 'Iconography of Sunglasses'. We had many guest presenters including Bryan Dyches, who gave a compelling presentation on 'Trends in Retail Experience'. The highlight of the summit was the 'Music, Fashion & Branding' panel that included some of the most innovative minds in the industry: Tim Scanlin (Brandracket), Lindsay Harris and Julianne Johnson (Viva La Rock), Charissa Saverio (DJ Rap), and Valida (KCRW, Standard Hotel). Each day wrapped with an exclusive music performance as LA indie rockers NO and Blondire stopped by, chatted and played intimate acoustic sets. On top of all that, we got the VIP treatment from Indians who were performing at The Echo. For the third year straight, I engaged with Sunglass Hut on how music can strengthen their brand and I am looking forward to many more.

Our work with Sunglass Hut has truly helped strengthen the brand's relationship with their consumers. Fisher concludes with: 'Frankly, music and sunglasses go hand in hand, don't you think?' I could not agree more.

Chapter 7

MUSIC AS CURRENCY

BY ERIC SHEINKOP

SINCE THE START OF THE 21st century, we've witnessed an onslaught of new technologies, companies and business models that although may provide different services, have been working congruently to produce a massive disruption in two industries which have always relied heavily on one another: music and advertising. During this time, nearly everything about how people communicate with one another, access information and arrive at purchasing decisions has evolved. This has tremendous implications for the current and future methods by which brands seek to reach their target demographics.

As the old saying goes, 'You can't know where you're going unless you know where you've been.' So, in an effort to help you more fully understand the future partnership model for brands and music, let us first rewind to the golden age of record labels, explore why this partnership first began, highlight the powers that allowed for the partnership to flourish and then discuss the occurrences that have since led to the virtual demise of the traditional model.

Originally, the only way to discover new music was through record labels. In their golden age, they controlled the music market in its entirety. Today they play a much smaller role and have lost a significant degree of relevance in the new music landscape. It is this transformation of the role of the record label that has opened up creative opportunities for artist and music inclusion and created a considerable paradigm shift in how brands and the music and advertising industries interact with one another.

RECORD LABEL KINGS

Since their inception in the late 1800s until roughly the start of the 21st century, record labels had the power to make and deliver on myriad promises to new artists, all hungry for a slice of the fame and fortune pie enjoyed by their idols. Labels enjoyed decades of supremacy by consolidating the power of various facets of the music industry within themselves. In so doing, they were able to keep the barriers of entry into the industry high. So high, in fact, that for years it was nearly impossible for an artist to have his or her music heard on any type of large scale without being signed to, and effectively owned by, a record label.

Record labels created for themselves, and for the music industry as a whole, a business model in which they – not the artists – were at the epicenter. For as long as traditional radio and manufactured products such as vinyls, eight-tracks, cassettes and especially CDs were the preferred and only methods for public consumption and purchase of music, record labels dominated. Artists were knocking down their doors, clamoring for meetings with label executives in hopes of cashing in on the promises on which labels were delivering for many of their peers. A record label provided artists with unprecedented access to resources such as studio time and the ability to work with professional recording engineers. Record labels were also able to mass-produce the physical music product by pressing records to vinyl, so controlled the music supply chain in such a way that they were able to ensure placement of these records on store shelves. Once they placed these records in prime retail space, record labels had enough capital to fund massive promotional campaigns. This meant that for one album a record label could secure radio play and television advertisements, billboard space and appearances by the artists on the most popular television programs. Therefore, even if an artist could secure enough funds to record independently, they could never perform the other operations that record labels had streamlined. They would still need to find some way to get their records in stores, not to mention head up their own publicity and advertising campaign to convince the public these albums were worth buying. It was this absolute control of all the facets of the music industry that made record labels so powerful. Artists *needed* record labels if they had any hope of becoming successful. By covering the costs of production, manufacturing, distribution, marketing and advertising of their music, record labels offered artists a road to stardom paved with gold…and groupies.

With little or no competition, record labels presented a pretty great product offering to artists aspiring for rock star status. If an artist could shore up enough money to put together a demo decent enough to prove his or her potential value to a label, he or she would be 'rewarded' with a record deal. These deals presented struggling artists with (often sorely needed) loans up front and access to thousand-dollar-an-hour studios. They would even have access to their very own production team determined to transform that demo from potential into actual value. When the product was ready to be brought to market, again the record label assumed responsibility, because it owned the control. But this control over the market that record labels created did not happen overnight. It was a product of decades of dominance over distribution channels and music marketing strategy. In 'Cycles in Symbol Production: The Case of Popular Music', Richard Peterson and David Berger explain that the four major record labels from 1948 to 1955 – RCA Victor, Columbia, Decca and Capitol – developed a model of vertical integration to create and maintain this complete control over the entry into the music industry. It was not the fact that these labels were providing the consumer with music that catered to their tastes, but rather that they controlled the entire distribution process of music. So, in essence, record labels first molded consumers' music tastes, then created and controlled the entire market for these tastes.

There were two important phases in creating and maintaining this control over the market. First was the control of music production and distribution. Each of these major labels owned a slew of record storage warehouses and wholesale dealerships. This control at the first step of the distribution process gave them almost complete control over all record stores, including independents. They could essentially hold these retail spaces to ransom because 'they could discourage individual retailers from handling the records of independent companies by threatening to delay shipments of their own most fast-moving records.'[1]

The second phase of this quest for control involved the marketing of the actual record. The Big Four record labels also happened to have extremely close ties with major media companies that owned various radio station syndicates in the United States. For example, RCA Victor actually created the first major broadcast network in the United States when it formed NBC in 1926, so it is no surprise that RCA had a great deal of control over what NBC was broadcasting over its airwaves. Columbia also had its own network, CBS. The reason these labels leveraged these close ties with radio stations was simple. Radio was the only free form of music consumption available at the time, and therefore was the major source of new music discovery for consumers.

Clearly, under this old model, radio represented the most effective channel for widespread exposure to new music. At their zenith, record labels represented the sole source for new and hot music for local radio station DJs. By positioning themselves as tastemakers capable of consistently delivering music that would keep listener figures high among stations' target demographics, and thus advertisers happy, record labels were able to create a need for their product within the very institution upon which its own success was predicated. While the major labels provided DJs with the musical resources that were essential for a radio station's survival, they did not always have absolute control and influence over the DJ and the content of the station. After all, these majors were still in competition with one another. Columbia had to make sure its artists were getting more airplay than artists from Capitol. This was the best way to ensure Columbia would experience more record sales than Capitol. Unsurprisingly, therefore, record label employees responsible for promoting their artists' new music worked closely with radio DJs during this time to secure radio play. DJs were the ones who actually played the music on the station, and therefore were an invaluable resource to labels. When the labels did not have direct control over the radio affiliate as in the case of RCA and NBC or Columbia and CBS, they had to resort to other means in order to persuade the DJ to promote their artists.

This gave rise to a practice termed payola, or 'pay for play'. Essentially, this method involved bribing DJs to play the record label's artists on the air. Since record labels at this time had virtually unlimited funds, this practice was easy to execute and became commonplace. Not only did payola help guarantee a record's increased airplay and therefore higher sales, it also helped an album soar in the charts. These charts ranked airplay and thus the popularity of a song or album, so a song that was getting played on the radio a great deal could make it into the Top 40 charts. Because the public highly valued these charts, a song or album in them would experience a boost in sales, which, after all, was the ultimate goal of the labels. The Federal Communications Commission deemed payola illegal in 1960 in the United States and many countries followed suit immediately after. Despite the government outlawing payola, the practice continued for several decades. Since these payments were made under the table they were difficult, if not impossible, to track. Knowing how quick and effective this practice was in building a song's popularity, label executives were willing to pay fines and face legal ramifications. In fact, in 1998 Interscope Records paid a Portland, Oregon radio station $5000 to play one Limp Bizkit song 50 times over a five-week period in order to send the song up the charts (*The New York Times*, 1998)[2]. This proved that as long as radio dominated as the one and only source for new music, record labels would dominate radio.

Remember, at this time, radio was still the only channel for public discovery of new music and people purchased CDs, not downloads (feels like forever ago, doesn't it?). So if labels controlled the music being played on the radio, and increased radio play led to higher CD sales, which represented the highest profit margins for the record labels, why would they ever want this business model to change? They had no choice. The perfect world that record labels had created and controlled was slowly dissolved, and for them to have even a fighting chance of keeping their doors open, they had to find new outlets, new platforms and new partners.

ADVERTISING HISTORY

At the same time that record labels were experiencing their heyday, so was the advertising agency. The post-Civil War era brought about a resurgence in American newspapers, and with them, prime real estate for advertisements. People could advertise anything from a particular skill set, all the way to chickens, for prices as low as 10 cents in papers with large circulations such as the *New York Observer*. These low prices made for a great deal of competition. Ads with large amounts of text that described the product were therefore quickly dropped in favor of catchy slogans that would stick in the consumer's head. For example, Kodak's 'You press the button, we do the rest' slogan was one of the first catchy one-liners used by a major company to grab the consumer's attention and gain their business. In 1893 Frank Munsey's magazine *Munsey* was the first to introduce low-priced issues of just 10 cents. Munsey was able to undersell the competition because he decided to make advertising the main source of revenue for his magazine, not subscriptions. In the years that followed, all major publications began to adopt this revenue model, and the long-term relationship between advertising and media was born.

The advertising industry was again transformed when radio appeared on the scene in the 1920s. Consumers across the globe tuned into their local radio stations for their news as well as entertainment. Companies often sponsored popular radio shows in order to pay for production costs and airtime. This is evident in shows like *The Voice of Firestone* or the *Bell Telephone Hour*, both of which featured classical music. Simply by sponsoring a radio show, companies like Firestone and Bell were able to gain unheard-of exposure thanks to this new mass communication device. When companies did not have the resources to secure their business's name in the title of the radio program through radio show sponsorship, they enlisted the narrators of the radio shows to read their product advertisements. Because radio represented the first and, at the time, only mass broadcasting device, radio show presenters gained a great deal of cachet among consumers and were very often considered celebrities in their own right. This was the beginning of product endorsements. If a consumer tuned in to listen to their favorite radio star, they would certainly be swayed by the star's opinion when he or she recommended purchasing a specific product.

As new technologies were developed that altered public media consumption habits, the advertising industry had to be quick to respond and adapt. Again, the advertising game changed in the 1950s with the introduction of television. Now commercials needed to have visual appeal. Advertisers still relied on celebrity endorsements in commercial breaks during popular programs, but with the advent of the videotape in 1956, advertisers were now able to film commercials for later and repeated playback. This new technology, along with the introduction of color television in 1965, brought with them a host of previously untapped creative possibilities in advertising and ushered in a new era of product advertising. Unlike traditional print or radio advertisements, which were designed to be more fact-based, television commercials allowed companies to appeal to consumers by selling a lifestyle and not simply product facts. This meant much higher production values and required even more succinct messaging on the part of advertisers. Not only this, but television shows led to a more enthralled and engaged audience. Television programs would often stop a storyline at its climax, leaving a 'cliffhanger' and going to a commercial break. Because the viewer did not want to miss the most exciting part of the television show, he or she was almost guaranteed to watch all of the commercials while waiting in anticipation of the show's return.

The most important factor in the success of advertising during the pre-dotcom boom was that brands had an easily accessible, captive audience. The consumer base was hand-delivered to brands by newspapers, radio programs and television shows. All the advertisers had to do was figure out which papers or shows their target demographic liked and read or tuned into regularly. By placing advertisements in these papers or during these shows, they would easily reach their consumer base. But as more channels and media outlets began to emerge, it became increasingly difficult for advertisers to identify where their target consumers were and how they could best reach them to make an impact. Although new outlets and technologies created more opportunities for brands and advertisers to connect with their audiences, it also led to increased consumer choice and a more fragmented media landscape, forcing brands to begin looking for new outlets, platforms and partners to help make an impact on consumers.

NEW TECHNOLOGIES: RECORD LABEL DISTRIBUTION DISRUPTION AND ADVERTISING IMPLICATIONS

Now let us fast-forward a bit, to a time that more closely resembles how we live today. In the late 1990s, technologies began to spring up that threw a wrench into this whole model – for record labels as well as the advertising industry and the brands they supported. These technologies proved to be especially disruptive for record labels, as they essentially altered every aspect of the labels' business model, rendering their entire process useless. Remember, the reason labels were able to rake in billions a year at the height of their success was by controlling these various music business processes: production, manufacturing, distribution and marketing – especially the distribution of music. When Napster – the first, and arguably most significant of these disruptive technologies – came on the scene, labels lost control of their distribution channel. It no longer mattered that record labels owned massive storage spaces for physical albums and CDs. It did not matter that they could force record stores to stock their labels' albums. The internet brought about the end of the physical music product and, therefore, an end to overly inflated label prices. Naturally, people seized the opportunity to keep some money in their pockets by downloading free music from the internet instead of purchasing CDs as they had in the past. Not only did Napster and similar services introduce the new accessibility of free music, it also allowed consumers for the first time to access individual tracks without owning the entire album. Add to that the meteoric rise of MP3 players and iPods, and you've got some serious distribution disruption and record-label profit losses. Things got even dicier once sites like Myspace, imeem, Last.fm and Pandora crept their way into the public domain, and people realized that radio (which up until this point the labels had controlled) was no longer the only avenue by which to listen to free music and discover new artists. For the first time ever, labels didn't have control over what people chose to listen to.

The real problem for the record labels did not emerge simply because Napster came onto the scene. It was the record label response to Napster and all of the subsequent new disruptive technologies that caused them to dig their own grave. Rather than adapting to, and embracing this new technology, the labels simply stuck to their old business models and launched a series of legal attacks against not only the disruptive technology companies, but the consumers using the new services as well. Essentially, record labels were hoping to bully consumers back into their old music consumption patterns. As soon as these disruptive technologies began to affect consumer trends, the Record Industry Association of America (RIAA), a trade group representing the entire recorded music industry, including all the major labels, attempted to reverse these trends back in their favor. The RIAA launched several public education campaigns discouraging the public from downloading from Napster and similar services, they increased funding to special interest groups in order to get protective legislation passed in Congress and brought legal action against the companies and consumers that threatened their power.

The second Napster entered the stage it changed consumer behavior. Napster gave users not only free music and more choice, but instant music. However, instead of copying this behavioral model of digitally downloadable music, or attempting to work with the new technologies to devise a solution for navigating this new digital landscape, the music industry sat back for an entire three years before developing a means by which to reconfigure their product in a new online music model.[3]

This solution, as we all know, was iTunes. It copied all the behavioral queues of Napster with one difference. Users now had to pay for this music. If this model had been introduced at Napster's onset, perhaps it could have had a chance. But after three years of downloading music for free, consumers were set in their ways and they were not about to start paying now. Once consumers are introduced to a behavior-altering new technology, especially one that allows for an enhanced and more efficient user experience, there is very little likelihood of them reverting to their old ways. Industries must adapt to changing consumer demands, not the converse.

It is no surprise that we still live in an age where the consumer believes music should be free. In fact, only 44 percent of US internet users, and 64 percent of Americans who purchase digitally, think that music is worth paying for, according to a study conducted by Forrester Research. Illegally downloaded music continues to account for 90 percent of the overall market.[4]

People are still buying music, but not nearly on the scale that they were during the record industry's golden years. 2011 was the first year ever that digital music sales accounted for a greater percentage of purchases than physical sales, according to the Neilsen and *Billboard* magazine's 2011 Music Industry Report.[5]

In 2011 consumers bought 1.27 billion digital tracks. This accounted for 50.3 percent of all music sales. While digital music sales increased by 8.5 percent, sales of physical CDs fell by 20 percent. This caused the overall retail music market's sales to fall 10.9 percent to nearly $6.9 billion. Clearly by the time the record industry switched to the digital model it was too late. Yes, digital sales have finally overtaken physical sales, but they are not nearly as profitable as the industry would hope.

With the industry as a whole hemorrhaging more and more money every year, a record deal is no longer the path to fame and fortune for an artist that it once was. Remember those loans that the record companies would so kindly give to struggling artists for a chance to turn their rough demo into a platinum album? Well, when their artists' CDs were selling for $14.00, labels had no problem recouping this money. With the album market getting crushed by consumers purchasing individual tracks for just 99 cents, return on record label investments has dwindled significantly. However, it is not just the aging out of these record label giants that is causing the industry's drastic transformation. The introduction of Napster and similar services has digitized public consumption of music and expanded free, instant access to a world of new music created without record label support. So where is all of this new music coming from and what are the implications for consumers?

NEW TECHNOLOGIES AND THE EXPANSION OF CHOICE

Much in the same way that music consumption experienced a digital revolution, so too has music creation. The leaps and bounds made in music production technology in recent years allow pretty much anyone with a MacBook to be a 'bedroom producer' and self-proclaimed rockstar. Access to high-quality production technology used to be doled out to select artists at the discretion of the major labels, ensuring they controlled the creation of new music. Today, this type of software comes standard with any new computer or can be downloaded for a nominal fee, and can be easily manipulated to make quality music. Couple this with the explosion of online services such as YouTube, SoundCloud, Bandcamp and others, which provide free, quick and easy platforms to make your music available to pretty much anyone at any time, and it makes sense that the music industry landscape has changed drastically.

Savvy artists today understand that instead of spending an exorbitant amount of time trying to get noticed by a label in hopes of landing a record deal, they have all of the necessary platforms themselves for creation, distribution and exposure of their music to launch a successful career. And instead of losing rights to their music as they would with a record label, artists who chart their own path to success maintain full rights and thus are able to reap higher profit margins than they would with a record deal.

We live in an age where the Rebecca Blacks and Carly Rae Jepsens of the world can record a song in their bedroom, make a music video with their friends, and then become a YouTube sensation and household name. You don't have to buy an album, you can just use Google to find a torrent, or save yourself a step and just stream it on Spotify. If you want your friend to hear a new band, you don't have to spend an hour dubbing a cassette tape, you just post a link to it on their Facebook Timeline. If you can't make it to a concert, you can watch it on your computer from the comfort of your own living room for free thanks to services like Livestream, a live streaming video platform that allows users to view and broadcast video content using a camera and a computer through the internet.

Whereas record labels once created ridiculously high barriers to enter the industry, these technological developments have lowered the bar so much that the internet is flooded with artists creating, distributing and marketing every type of music you can imagine and probably a lot that you cannot.

According to the International Federation of the Phonographic Industry (IFPI), in 2011, Myspace alone had:

- 2.5 million registered hip-hop acts
- 1.8 million rock acts

- 720,000 pop acts and
- 470,000 punk acts.

And as of 2012, iTunes had over 28 million available songs,[6] Bandcamp has 4,801,877 tracks and 595,412 albums,[7] Spotify has a catalogue of over 15 million songs, and Pandora has a stockpile of about 800,000 songs.[8]

Now that is a lot of music. While at first glance, this may seem like every music lover's dream, this flooded music marketplace actually creates problems for consumers. The first and most basic problem is the amount of time it takes a person to sift through all this information to find the next big thing, or even just finding new music with which they connect. The more complex issue relates to the mental burden a person deals with when faced with too much choice.

In his work, *The Paradox of Choice*, social psychologist Barry Schwartz argues that, while it may feel counterintuitive, a person's level of happiness and overall satisfaction increases as personal choice decreases. He points to two experiments performed by Sheena Iyengar and Mark Lepper to illustrate his point:

> One study was set in a gourmet food store in an upscale community where, on weekends, the owners commonly set up sample tables of new items. When researchers set up a display featuring a line of exotic, high-quality jams, customers who came by could taste samples, and they were given a coupon for a dollar off if they bought a jar. In one condition of the study, 6 varieties of the jam were available for tasting. In another, 24 varieties were available. In either case, the entire set of 24 varieties was available for purchase. The large array of jams attracted more people to the table than the small array, though in both cases people tasted about the same number of jams on average. When it came to buying, however, a huge difference became evident. Thirty percent of the people exposed to the small array of jams actually bought a jar; only 3 percent of those exposed to the large array of jams did so.

In a second study, this time in the laboratory, college students were asked to evaluate a variety of gourmet chocolates, in the guise of a marketing survey. The students were then asked which chocolate – based on description and appearance – they would choose for themselves. Then they tasted and rated that chocolate. Finally, in a different room, the students were offered a small box of the chocolates in lieu of cash as payment for their participation. For one group of students, the initial array of chocolates numbered 6, and for the other, it numbered 30. The key results of this study were that the students faced with the small array were more satisfied with their tasting than those faced with the large array. In addition, they were four times as likely to choose chocolate rather than cash as compensation for their participation.[9]

Schwartz's argument that eliminating consumer choices can lead to decreased levels of anxiety and mental burden can be understood in our context as the consumer's need for fewer music choices. In the past, major record labels provided the public with a music filtering mechanism by way of their radio control. A teenager looking to find the hot new songs of the week used to be able to just flip on the radio and listen to their favorite radio station's Top 10 list. However, according to Nielsen's August 2012 'Music 360' report,[10] US teens today prefer to listen to music via YouTube:

- 64 percent of teens listen to music through YouTube
- 56 percent of teens listen to music on the radio
- 53 percent of teens listen to music through iTunes
- 50 percent of teens listen to music on CD.

And with 72 hours of video uploaded to YouTube every minute, even if half of that content is music-related, it is safe to say that the choices are endless. Teens today lack the filter that a radio station's Top 10 list used to provide, but also the myriad online music blogs and forums representing themselves as the experts, who all have differing opinions on what constitutes 'cool' music, complicate things. The consumer would benefit from a music filter provided by a trusted source that has taken the time to understand their passions, wants and motivations. These new technologies that have led to a massive influx of newly available and instantly accessible music have had a detrimental effect on the music industry. They have created a host of new mental burdens for today's consumers, but also provided an enormous opportunity for brands to step in as partners of the new music industry, and of their target demographics as well, by becoming a tool for music discovery and filtering for its consumers.

NEW TECHNOLOGIES AND ADVERTISING IMPLICATIONS

But the music industry does not exist in a vacuum. Since the beginning of the 21st century, new technologies have become available that have also had a significant impact on the advertising industry, as they have completely revolutionized the ways in which people consume media and receive brand messages.

Brands' ability to reach and engage their target audiences, as well as the advertising agencies tasked to do so, were crippled by the rise of internet sites like Hulu, YouTube and Netflix as well as the introduction of technologies such as satellite radio, TiVo, On Demand, DVRs and Sky+. Rapidly declining radio listeners, coupled with technologies whose primary value proposition is allowing consumers to bypass commercials, has made it tougher than ever for brands to reach their audiences.

A more recent thorn in the sides of advertisers has been the growing popularity of 'connected TV viewing.' In July 2012, The Pew Research Center's Internet & American Life Project[11] found that just over half of all adult cell phone owners (52 percent) have used their phones recently for engagement, diversion or interaction with other people while watching TV:

- 38 percent of cell phone owners used their phone to keep themselves occupied during commercials or breaks in something they were watching
- 23 percent used their phone to exchange text messages with someone else who was watching the same program in a different location
- 22 percent used their phone to check whether something they heard on television was true
- 20 percent used their phone to visit a website that was mentioned on television
- 11 percent used their phone to see what other people were saying online about a program they were watching, and 11 percent posted their own comments online about a program they were watching using their mobile phone
- 6 percent used their phone to vote for a reality show contestant.

Some of the most interesting statistics from the survey are two of the above points that when taken together would seem to contradict one another, but are actually indicative of how the consumer–advertiser relationship is evolving. On the one hand, the Pew survey found that 38 percent of cell phone owners used their phones to keep themselves occupied during commercials or when there was a break in the content they were watching. This would seem to suggest a complete lack of engagement on the part of the consumer with anything beyond the TV show they are watching at the time. However, the same survey found that 20 percent of viewers used their cell phone to visit a website that was mentioned on the screen. Whether that website mention occurred during the actual TV show or a commercial is less important than the fact that a simple mention garners a 20 percent direct engagement with that site, as it is clearly indicative that the consumer and brand relationship has moved, in a very serious way, to mobile and online. This shift to the crowded digital landscape means that advertisers will continue to lose control of their once captive audiences, as the online world brings with it infinite options and consumer freedom through new technologies by which to access it.

Whereas record labels dug themselves deeper into a hole by spending millions of dollars trying to combat these new technologies, advertisers have followed their consumers right to the platforms on which they are spending time. Brands and advertisers have reallocated ad spend away from TV, newspapers, magazines and radio and turned to digital platforms in an attempt to stay connected to their consumer base. US online advertising spending, which grew 23 percent to $32.03 billion in 2011, is expected to grow an additional 23.3 percent to $39.5 billion within a year. This will push it ahead of total spending on print newspapers and magazines.

If advertisers are cutting traditional ad spending by staggering amounts, then where exactly are their advertising dollars? Advertisers are adapting to this changing technology and putting their money toward tactics that directly connect them with targeted consumers. These include search marketing, online video, social media and direct marketing. The bottom line is that these new ways of connecting with the consumer take place online. For the advertising industry to survive, it had to adapt. Traditional media alone will no longer cut it. Emarketer, a company specializing in advertising industry analysis, predicts that digital will be the primary beneficiary of an industry-wide shift in marketing dollars away from traditional channels like TV, radio and print. The company predicts that by the year 2016, US advertisers will spend $62 billion on online advertising – double what they spent in 2011 – while TV ad spending will see moderate increases in spending, and print advertising will actually decrease from $36 billion in 2011 to just over $32 billion in 2016.[12]

MAJOR LABELS AND ADVERTISERS: THE ENEMY OF MY ENEMY IS MY FRIEND

With their once captive audiences dwindling, and budgets right along with them, brands and advertisers have been forced to find new ways to get their message in front of consumers. As the previously presented information shows, a means by which to do this has been a reallocation of ad spend toward digital platforms. Another way that brands and advertisers sought to beat back the detrimental effect of new technologies on their ability to reach consumers was by more fully embracing music. For years they sought to leverage its unprecedented emotion-evoking power to create more distinctive and real connections between brands and their target demographics. It has always been something of a natural partnership, but not necessarily one that was viewed as mutually beneficial for both the brands and the artists.

For example, in the early 1970s Paul Simon recorded the song 'Going Home' for his upcoming album, *There Goes Rhymin' Simon*. He later decided that 'Going Home' was too generic a song name, and chose instead to change the name of the track to 'Kodachrome'. Those of you who remember life before digital cameras became as ubiquitous as they are today will likely remember that Kodachrome was one of Kodak's first color films.

'They give us those nice bright colors. They give us the greens of summers. Makes you think all the world's a sunny day,' Simon sang. '... So Mama don't take my Kodachrome away.'[13]

Fearing the term 'Kodachrome' would make its way into popular vernacular as a generic term for film, in the same way that Frigidaire was used at the time to refer to refrigerators, Kodak pressed Simon to revert back to the song's original title. After much back and forth, Kodak finally agreed to let Simon keep the title, but only if it accompanied a disclaimer that Kodachrome was a registered trademark of Kodak.[14]

It wasn't until the early 1990s, when both the advertising and music industries began to experience changes, that they began to look to one another as a means by which to better engage their consumers and raise their bottom lines. Although major record labels were becoming less relevant as their power dwindled, advertisers knew they could still be counted on to deliver star power for a campaign.

Eager to regain their footing in the industry and find new revenue streams to replace their failing traditional profit-making avenues, major record labels were more than willing to offer up their roster of already established household-name artists with whom brands could partner.

It was a no-brainer for brands and advertisers. They viewed partnerships with major label mainstays as the quickest fix for the conundrum with which they were faced. Music offered brands and advertisers a way to stay relevant and fresh with their target audience, and major labels hoped this would be the opportunity they had been looking for to reline their pockets with money they were losing from traditional album sales. With that, music and brands went from casually dating to married with three kids – and we see the offspring of this marriage every day.

Successful brands know their audiences and look for synergies with other brands that cater to similar people. It's hard to look around and not see a partnership forming at any given time: Jay-Z and Duracell; Nicki Minaj and Pepsi; Madonna and Louis Vuitton and Dolce & Gabbana; Jennifer Lopez and L'Oréal; Justin Timberlake and Givenchy; The Black Eyed Peas and…anything with a paycheck. All of these artists are well-developed 'brands' in themselves. They each already have built-in target audiences that align with the products or services they choose to endorse. What was once considered 'selling out' by artists 10 or 15 years ago has now come to be expected and today, artists who have not found a brand with which to align will find themselves fighting an even steeper uphill battle to success.

Realistically, this type of major label celebrity endorsement strategy will never fully disappear. However, in the past few years, we've begun to see the smartest brands align themselves with more independent, up-and-coming, buzzworthy artists. Partnerships like Chevy and Fun; Apple and Feist; Lowe's and Gin Wigmore; and Toyota's Scion and the Melvins all provide evidence of this indie-artist shift.

And why is this? First of all, if a famous song, and especially one that we hear all day on the radio, like 'I Gotta Feeling', is put into an ad, it usually fades to the background: no one notices it, let alone will talk about how great an ad it was. They already know the song, and hearing it repurposed in an advertisement becomes overkill. From a brand's perspective, it also tends to be costly, time-consuming and laden with headache-inducing legalities.

Licensing music is an intricate and costly process, and the more established the artist whose music one is attempting to license, the more complicated the process becomes. Music licensing is a multistage process, which includes researching the owner of various copyrights, obtaining clearances and quotes, and negotiating, drafting and revising the licensing agreement. For a brand, this process can be inconvenient because it can take anywhere from a few days to as long as months. In extreme conditions, it is sometimes impossible for a brand even to get their hands on the rights to the song. An artist may not want to be associated with the particular brand or they may fear that a brand sponsorship will exclude them from possible opportunities in the future. Because of this, licensing music from high-profile artists is sometimes very difficult and not cost-effective.[15]

Sponsoring a major name artist's tour is also nice in theory. But when we break it down it becomes easy to see that this in fact does not work to establish brand equity. A brand wants to create goodwill with their demographic. They want their clientele to think they are ahead of the curve. They hope any partnership with a musical act will cause their audience to think and speak about them favorably.

What's more likely to happen in this scenario is that the band overshadows and eclipses the brand and product. People will be back at work or school the next day and talking about those bizarre neon bulbs Will.i.am was wearing or Fergie's push-up bra – they most certainly will not be talking about that corporate sponsor whose ads were draped across the stage. Chances are they will not have even noticed the ads or given them a second thought. This sort of advertising has become too routine and can be easily ignored.

Now, on the other hand, if a brand throws a great party or concert with a few unknown, upcoming or buzzworthy acts, the *brand* becomes a tastemaker, and is what gets talked about the next day around the water cooler or in the lunchroom. And this is because it is a point of reference when telling the story. People will say, 'I went to the coolest event last night, 'X' Brand threw a party and had all these really great new acts I haven't heard of before. They gave me a CD on the way out and it's incredible. You've got to hear it.' That's a far better and more cost-effective way for a brand to create unique and authentic touchpoints with an audience rather than paying to be overshadowed.

SOCIAL EMPOWERMENT: THE FUTURE BRAND AND CONSUMER INTERACTION MODEL

Now that we have explored a bit of the recent past in the music and advertising industries and the myriad challenges within each that have been driven by a host of new technologies, let us look at what the future holds. While it is undeniable that technology played a starring role in the destruction of traditional business models, it has also provided new tools that can be leveraged to create better, more profitable and sustainable industries. It has created opportunities for new revenue streams for brands, labels and artists, as well as access to deeper and richer music experiences for consumers.

Consumers today have access to unlimited content and can connect with the world in an instant. According to a 2012 Neilsen report tracking American media consumption habits, almost 75 percent of US households owned four or more televisions. The study also found that 290 million Americans and 114.7 million households owned at least one. This is coupled with 211 million Americans who have internet access using a computer and 116 million with internet access on a mobile device. So what happens when Americans own so many devices that keep them connected? What happens is that they consume a whole lot of content. In 2011 the average American spent nearly 42 hours per week watching video content across all platforms: traditional TV, personal video recorded TV, internet on the computer and internet on a mobile device.

Clearly, consumers today experience some serious information overload. Naturally these circumstances make it difficult for people to turn this information overload into meaningful experiences that improve their lives. So how can brands and advertisers connect with their target audiences most effectively amid this overcrowded, hyperactive information landscape?

THE ANSWER IS SOCIAL EMPOWERMENT

Social Empowerment is a sustainable marketing model whereby a brand can organically insert itself into a consumer's everyday life, beyond its product or service. At the root of this model is an understanding and appreciation for passions that exist among a brand's target audience. These passion points can include music, sports, gaming, fashion or even technology. But right now we are going to focus on music and how marketers can leverage it in a way that empowers their consumers to become tastemakers in their personal circles, and ultimately form meaningful and long-lasting relationships with brands.

Study after study has shown the myriad effects that music has on the human brain. According to a study by Valorie Salimpoor of McGill University in Montreal,[16] listening to music produces an enormous cognitive response. Salimpoor and his team conducted numerous experiments in which they monitored subjects' brain activity in an MRI scanner while the subjects listened to music. Participants experienced a variety of effects such as increased heart rate and respiration. But the most important finding of this study was not the physiological effects of the music, but the cognitive ones. Subjects that listened to music experienced a 6 to 21 percent increase in dopamine levels in the brain during the experiments compared to the control group, which did not experience this increase. Dopamine is a chemical released by the body when we do something our brains want us to do again. Dopamine creates a feeling of pleasure and is therefore emitted when we do things that we typically associate with a positive emotional state like having sex, eating our favorite foods or doing drugs. For example, a person on cocaine experiences about a 20 percent increase in dopamine. Cocaine specifically binds to receptors of brain cells, which keeps the brain from processing dopamine. Therefore, dopamine levels in the brain remain extremely high when someone is on this drug. This is extremely important because this means that music affects the brain so intensely that it naturally mirrors this chemically induced state.

While scientists are undecided on why exactly our minds respond to music in this way, there is a large school of thought that thinks this is actually an evolutionary response. A study by Stanford professor, Vinod Menon, found that the patterns in music naturally create a feeling of anticipation in the listener. A person can follow the melody and guess what comes next, but it is this waiting and predicting that creates a sense of urgency and eagerness. This study found that during short breaks or climaxes in songs, there is a great deal of brain activity in the listener, suggesting that they are paying extremely close attention to what will come next. Because music engages the brain over time through this process of starts, stops, climaxes and hooks, 'this process of listening to music could be the way that the brain sharpens its ability to anticipate events and sustain attention.'[17] These two studies are important because they show that music has two profound effects on the human brain: it creates an enormous sense of pleasure in the brain and also helps sustain attention. Therefore, using music in branding strategy is basically a marketer's dream. Music makes consumers happy and makes them pay attention. Science proves it.

The previously presented data on the use of streaming services and digital music purchases clearly illustrate an intense consumer/fan demand for music. People are constantly consuming music and today they have the technology to do it more easily than ever before. We have already seen that music is scientifically proven to create positive emotional states in human beings, which helps to explain why people spend so much of their time listening to music. However, if this were the only factor, people would not feel the need to consume so many different types of music on the scale that we are seeing today. They could simply buy a few albums they like, listen to them over and over, and experience the pleasurable state this music creates in their brains. The reason people do not experience music in this way is because music, and the culture surrounding it, doesn't just provide cognitive benefits, but social as well. As seen in the previous research, music is a universal connector, motivator and reward-center activator, the result of an evolutionary adaptation. Because of this, music affects everyone and it is no surprise that it is a topic of many conversations. But there are many different types of music, and therefore many different groups of people who enjoy and talk about a specific genre of music. Having knowledge about a particular genre or band is a golden ticket into particular social circles because it is a shared interest. Clearly, music provides for social inclusion. It gives you something to talk about and a common interest on which to base relationships. In addition to facilitating personal connections, knowledge about music also has the ability to separate people in a social setting. We've all been there – you're out with a group of people chatting about new music and someone mentions their new favorite artist. A couple of people chime in with their opinion on the artist, and those with no knowledge about that particular music are left on the periphery of the conversation and the new connections that blossom as a result of this shared musical knowledge.

Essentially, music entertains and fulfills a fan's desire to be cool within his or her own personal social circles. Everyone wants to be the first one to know about an awesome band. People love to say that they knew an artist *way* before they became famous, way before anyone else had even heard of them. In general, those in their social circle who have this special inside musical knowledge impress the others in the group. The others in the group want a piece of this knowledge as well because they share the same musical interests. Therefore, being the keeper of this knowledge and the first to find out about something new is admirable. Put more simply, it makes you cool. In the past, the way to achieve this social status was pretty simple. Be the kid who hangs out in the record store. Buy albums the first day they come out. Listen to a lot of music. The record labels, record stores and radio stations had already sifted through the muck to give you a small, tailored selection to 'search' through to find your new favorite band. All a person had to do was be the one who heard it first. Record label control assured that the vast majority of the music being pushed out into the public domain would become popular. That is just how it worked back then.

Today it is not quite that easy. With so much music available on the internet, it is nearly impossible to figure out who the next great artist is. Without record labels, record stores and radio stations filtering through this massive amount of music before it makes its way to the marketplace, how does the consumer even know where to start? The need to be the first to know about music, this need to be on the cusp of a trend and share it with your friends is nothing new, but the way to achieve this has become much more difficult. With infinite musical options, it is scarier than ever for a person – especially teens – to be the first to share new music with their circles. How can they be sure that this music will stand for them and truly reinforce their personal identities? How can they be sure that this music is in fact going to be considered 'cool' among this circle, when so many different blogs, forums and 'experts' have completely differing opinions?

This is where the opportunity for brands exists. While record labels no longer have the massive resources they once did to sift through the musical landscape and deliver a hit to a specifically identified audience, brands do. If a brand can consistently deliver cutting edge, tailored music to fans, whether through advertising or a specific online music discovery platform, then that brand fulfills the needs of the consumer. The consumer needs someone to be a filter for the music industry. They need to be presented with an amount of music that is digestible. Not only this, but they need to be presented with music that helps them maintain the trendy, well-informed status that they have in their social circle as well as help them connect with new types of people who share their interest in a particular artist or genre. If a brand can do this and the consumer can come to count on the brand to consistently deliver musical expertise that can be leveraged in the person's social setting, then in the eyes of the consumer, the brand becomes relevant and, more importantly, it becomes *useful*, beyond its product.

Let me break this down a bit more.

The consumer/fan has a desire and creates a demand for a specific type of music. With so many options out there, it is difficult and time-consuming for the fan to discover and fulfill this need on their own. Therefore, the fan looks to brands to use their vast resources to sift through the massive music scene and select the most relevant and therefore the most entertaining and fulfilling music for them. This provides a great opportunity for brands to fuel conversation. If they really understand the passion points of their consumers then they will provide their customers with music they want to talk about. Naturally, people want to share the new music they have discovered, to satisfy the social need to be the first to know, or even just stay relevant among colleagues and friends. If they found out about something because it was on a brand's website, or in a commercial, there is a great chance the brand will get the credit for introducing this consumer to a particular artist. In this way, the brand is now *meaningful* beyond its product. The brand is involved in everyday conversation, because its consumers are talking about music, and the brand was the one to introduce them to this music. This is the goal for a brand. While some brands have the power to interact with a consumer multiple times a day just by virtue of the product they sell, such as food or beverages, other brands whose product or service experiences a longer duration between purchases have less opportunity for inclusion in consumers' daily lives, and need to find ways to keep the conversation going between purchases. Music provides the opportunity for brands to have authentic and valuable between-purchase touchpoints with consumers.

To continue to occupy this role as musical curators, and thereby become important to the consumer in meaningful ways, beyond the product, brands will have to invest in artist discovery and development, stepping in to fill the void traditional record labels left after the industry collapse. In this way, brands are the curators, developers and providers of new music. Consumers now consistently begin to look to them for what's hot, and brands must continue to deliver or risk losing their engaged audience. This empowers fans to achieve the level of cool and social inclusion they aspire to, and includes them in the brand's new, hip music community. In return, the brand is now included in conversations and the everyday lives of consumers in a way that transcends brand loyalty. This deep connection based on passion points makes purchasing decisions a no-brainer when the eventual need for the physical product arises. The consumer is not going to choose the cheaper tennis shoe when they are finally due to upgrade their sneakers. They are going to choose the shoe brand that just spent the last few months introducing them to music that they not only loved, but music that helped them succeed in their social circle and make new friends. Record labels failed to create this type of loyalty and advocacy. When they lost control of the distribution process, consumers were more than happy to go to the cheaper (or free) options of Napster and other online music downloading services. It is irrelevant to a consumer whether their new music comes from Sony or a pop-up basement label because there is no sense of loyalty or connection to the major labels. Had the major labels truly connected with the consumer in a meaningful way, they could have maintained their customer base.

Today, brands are facing a similar problem. The marketplace is flooded with competition from other name brands and much cheaper generic brands. In order to rise above the clutter and win the business of the customer, the brand must connect with the consumer in a way that makes them important to the consumer's life. Consumers become so connected and even reliant, that they have no desire to buy the competing brand, even if it is cheaper. While we are in the midst of a distribution disruption for brands that is quite similar to the downfall of the record industry, they can still achieve success by using music to connect with the consumer. That way, when the cheaper sneakers come along, consumers will be unfazed.

They will want to buy the sneakers from the brand that understands them and helps them achieve their desired level of cool, knowing they can depend on the brand to constantly fuel them with new, relevant content.

In order to fulfill this desire of the fan to be cool, socially included and at the forefront of the music scene, the brand must first be connected with the consumer in a more personal and social way. This will allow the brand to tap into the fan's specific tastes and cater to them.

By understanding the consumer's passion points and motivations, the brand can develop a lasting relationship with the target audience. The reason that it is important to create and maintain this connection with consumers is simple. In this rapidly evolving marketplace made up of infinite choices, it is hard to tell what brands are worthy of your money. In a June 2012 survey conducted by About.com, 84 percent of consumers stated that they felt brands needed to prove themselves trustworthy before they would interact with them. The study went on to explain that consumers had their trust boosted in brands that provided them with some utility, or real benefit, and did not simply bombard them with sales pitches. These two ideas are vital in order for a brand to avoid becoming a victim of distribution disruption, and using a music-based marketing strategy is the best way to realize both of them. Music knowledge is useful to consumers because music provides a platform to develop relationships with other like-minded people. In addition, consumers utilize this music knowledge to help them become cool within their social circles. Clearly, the utility of music cannot be denied. These are real benefits. According to this model, providing useful information creates trust for the consumer. Since trust is needed for the consumer to interact with the brand, it is essential that brands gain this trust through provision of useful material, and music is an effective way to achieve this.

Like I said before, music is important, but not because there is a lack of music available to fans. On the contrary, there is so much that they cannot wrap their heads around it. As a curator of cool, a brand must figure out a way to choose music that adds value to the lives of the consumer. If it doesn't add value, fans are better off surfing music blogs and finding meaning for themselves.

It is no longer enough simply to give music away for free. Music is a passion point, meaning an area of interest that gets the consumer involved, excited and engaged. Therefore the brand must find unique and authentic ways to involve the consumer with the musical environment if they expect to rise above all the other noise and not simply push new tracks at them.

There are many ways to truly engage the consumer with music, especially with the various technologies now available. Brands can allow the consumer to remix tracks, be in music videos, or involve them in the creative process or even a unique show or experience. The brands that are able to create new, exciting and unique musical experiences for their consumers that enhance the communications and go beyond a free MP3, are the brands that truly engage with their customers and reap the benefits.

An effective example of a brand catering to the consumer's behavior in order to appeal to them is Vodafone UK's Booster Brolly. The Booster Brolly is an umbrella made up of solar panels that can be used to charge a cellphone. The eco-friendly umbrella uses the power of the sun to not only charge a mobile phone but to boost a 3G wireless signal. Vodafone introduced this product at the Isle of Wight Festival in order to help music fans stay in touch with one another as well as remain protected from Britain's rainy weather. This product provided the consumer with something useful, something that helps them do what they already do, but better. In this way, Vodafone is able to make a meaningful connection with the consumer.

Vodafone's Booster Brolly is indicative of the shift in how smart brands today market themselves to concertgoers. Live show sponsorship used to mean stamping a brand's logo on everything from the concert tickets and advertisements, to having branded signage on stage during the performance. As stated above, these types of positive association marketing tactics are highly ineffective means by which to build brand loyalty. Consumers today are smarter and have more choices than ever when it comes to purchasing products. The notion that a person is more likely to buy a product just because they saw a brand's logo plastered on a banner behind the band whose concert he or she attended last night, really has no place in today's marketing landscape.

Vodafone's Booster Brolly is a great example of how traditional live music sponsorship has evolved into more of a partnership. Instead of developing the Booster Brolly to get in front of their target demographic, Vodafone could simply have covered the festival grounds with their logo and hoped that consumers remembered them when it was time to buy a new cell phone. But they took it one step further and committed the additional resources necessary to develop an organic partnership.

By first understanding its consumers' passions – in this case music festivals – and then identifying their consumers' need for a better wireless signal, an easy way to charge their cell phone and shelter from Britain's sporadic rain showers, Vodafone was able to enhance its consumers' festival experience in a creative way. This method also stayed true to their brand and cemented a deeper relationship with its target demographic by being relevant to them beyond their product.

Another good example of Social Empowerment in practice is Coca-Cola's 2011 'Coke Music' campaign, an innovative music-centric marketing initiative focused on engaging with teens. Coke's problem was that they were losing touch with the younger generation. Coke was seen as the classic, boring soft drink, while Pepsi, along with other drink brands such as Dr Pepper and Monster, were young, exciting and popular with teens. In order to get teens interested in Coca-Cola again, Coke partnered with British indie rock quintet, One Night Only. This band was just emerging onto the scene when they recorded a track written by our team at Music Dealers called 'Can You Feel It' for Coke's new teen-focused campaign. Coke chose the band because of the upbeat, catchy, youthful feel of their music and potential teen appeal.

The idea behind the campaign was to give teens an inside look into the music scene by letting them see how the industry's leading artists work. Coke did this by creating an interactive music video for 'Can You Feel It' and posting it on their global music websites. On these sites, teens could upload their own videos of themselves. This footage was then integrated into the original video which allowed teens to see themselves with the band. Teens could then share the video on various social media sites, expanding the reach of the campaign through word-of-mouth promotion.

The reason this was successful was not just through the use of music, but due to the tailored, innovative use of a music platform that targeted a particular demographic. Coca-Cola tapped into not only *what type* of music (upbeat, catchy) teens liked to listen to but also *how* teens consumed and shared this music. Coke did not just give away a free MP3 because that is not how most teens get their music. They get new music from friends and through social media. Coke understood that it needed to appeal to this behavior. Making an interactive video is perfect because it is easy to share on social media and it is also personable. Friends wanted to share this video with other people not just because they liked the song, but because they themselves were in it, allowing them to showcase their identities across social networks. Coke didn't just create a music video and then expect teens to share it online. They understood that if they expected their audience to spread the content virally, the brand would have to create a unique musical experience that helped teens reinforce their identities among their circles. It is critical that a brand does not underestimate the courage it takes – especially for teens – to share something as personal as music on their social networks. In the days before Facebook, Twitter, Instagram and Tumblr, for example, sharing such content took place in person, say, at a party and among maybe five to ten friends. Today everyone seems to have magically accrued thousands upon thousands of 'friends' thanks to these new social networks, which means that the risk is much higher when sharing. Put simply, it takes some serious chutzpah to share content socially today.

By fully understanding the needs of their target teen audience and appreciating the vulnerability that accompanies sharing content on their social networks, Coke was able to execute an extremely successful campaign. Speaking in regard to the Coke Music project, Jonathan Mildenhall, Vice President of Global Advertising Strategy and Content Excellence at Coca-Cola, noted:

> The work created for 'Coca-Cola Music' is perhaps one of the broadest spreads of content that the Company has ever produced that has not been associated with a global event like the Olympics or the World Cup. Teens are the most demanding target audience as far as creativity is concerned and in the way they engage with a brand or campaign. They demand to interact and participate with brands and be a part of the conversation. This program has been designed with that understanding and to enable teens to view, participate and share the content and experiences.

The reason these approaches were successful is because they provide consumers with the resources and insider experiences they need to achieve their desired level of inclusion and relevance among their own social networks. In order to provide specific experiences to them it is extremely important that a brand understands its consumers' passion points, sphere of influence and the vulnerability experienced in their online world. If the brand experiences relate to their passions, consumers will gain something from the brand to help them reach their desired level of social inclusion, and therefore the brand will be viewed as valuable to the consumer beyond its product. This is the ultimate objective when employing Social Empowerment.

Chapter 8

CASE STUDIES FOR MUSIC AS CURRENCY

BY ERIC SHEINKOP

COCA-COLA

AS THE WORLD'S LARGEST BRAND, it is no surprise that Coca-Cola has dabbled in a wide variety of marketing efforts and techniques. Whether sponsoring sporting events, TV shows or environmental clean-up efforts, it is clear the company is constantly on the lookout for the next, most effective marketing strategy. Because of this innovative, cutting edge spirit, the brand has realized the power of more fully integrating music into its marketing strategy to address a recent challenge facing the company: Coca-Cola's loss of relevance and cachet among teenagers.

The use of music in Coca-Cola's marketing strategy is nothing new. Emmanuel Seuge, Coca-Cola's head of music and entertainment marketing, says that throughout its 125-year history the company has 'always paid very special attention to the type of music we are playing as a way to engage the conversation with its consumers'.

Seuge explains that music goes beyond simply catching the consumer's attention or providing background for a radio ad. It helps shape the identity of the brand and connects with the consumer.

Because of this, the continuously evolving music industry has helped form an integral part of Coca-Cola's brand image:

> From the very early days of the company, 120 years ago when we first started to use music and a musical singer Clark to do the advertising, down to Ray Charles in advertising in the 1960s, we have always collaborated with the music industry. We gave Ray Charles and Aretha Franklin an open brief to write our radio spots for us. We used their music expertise as a way for us to engage with our customers in different ways.

While leveraging music to create a strong brand image began over 100 years ago, Seuge says that today's approach to partnering with members of the music industry is quite different. He says that today, the brand looks at the music industry in a much more holistic way. Rather than partnering with one popular artist to provide the soundtrack for a quick TV spot, Coca-Cola is using artists and their music as a way of telling a story and connecting with the consumer on a new, deeper level.

> The reason why we have reengaged our music efforts three years ago on the global scale is that we have lost a lot of momentum with teenagers. For Coke to grow, it needs to grow its consumer base. We have not effectively recruited new teenagers since the early 2000s. We had to refigure how engaging our model with teens was and music was the best way to do that.

In order to connect with these teens on a deeper level, Seuge explains that Coke uses a two-pronged approach to musical marketing. The first part of the strategy is horizontal music integration. This means layering music into everything a brand does, meaning all advertising,

PR, social media and digital campaigns, as well as events. Through this use of musical branding, Coke is able to communicate with its audience at all steps through its marketing campaigns. Because there is music in everything Coke does, Coke is able to appeal to the consumer in each and every one of their marketing efforts.

According to Seuge, the second phase of a successful music-based marketing campaign is vertical integration. This means the music is more than simply a tune fading into the background of a commercial. Rather, the music is helping to tell a story and drive conversation.

> If you look on Facebook, music is one of the main if not the number one reason for people to share content and to engage in conversations with their friends. We need to be part of that conversation. If we want to be part of that conversation, we need to leverage music... We need to create content in the music world.

To do this, a brand must create stories through the use of music. But these are not just any stories. The stories must be authentic to the brand and also relevant to the consumer. One example of using music that is relevant to the consumer in order to draw in a new customer base is Coke's 2009 Open Happiness campaign. In an effort to appeal to teens, Coke organized the production of a track that featured artists who were extremely popular amongst teens at the time: Cee Lo Green of Gnarls Barkley, Patrick Stump from Fall Out Boy, Brendon Urie from Panic! at the Disco, Travis McCoy from Gym Class Heroes, and Janelle Monáe. In order to appeal to teens, the video for the song premiered on MTV and aired during commercials throughout the eighth season of American Idol. While the song itself was not particularly successful as far as *Billboard* numbers were concerned, Seuge explains that it taught Coke a great deal about the power of successful music marketing:

> The one thing that also helped show us internally is that music was the way to reach an audience in a different way and to reach the

audience that we would not capture through traditional advertising. All of a sudden we were creating content in the music world; because of that 'Open Happiness', we were talking to people that we had never spoken to before...certain types of consumers that are not into traditional advertising. All of a sudden music opened a bridge to talk to them that we have never done. Realizing that was a huge wake-up call saying, 'I realize the power of music.' I give much more credit to that song in terms of what it created after Coke than the result of the song itself...The point is that it proved in a unique target group how it allowed us to reach consumers in a way that we had not realized. All of a sudden music was something more than a sponsorship. Music was an integral part of our business.

Seuge says that it was this realization that paved the way for Coke's advertising strategy during the 2010 FIFA World Cup. The World Cup took place in South Africa and because of this, it was very important to Coke that they featured an African artist in their advertising campaign around the event. Through their search for an appropriate musician both to convey their message and appeal to their consumer base, Coke stumbled across K'naan, a Somalian-Canadian hip-hop artist.

They chose K'naan's song 'Wavin' Flag', an upbeat hip-hop track, because of its messages of coming together, freedom and patriotism. A remixed version of the song, 'Wavin' Flag Celebration Remix', was used in virtually all of Coca-Cola's World Cup international advertisements. In anticipation of the FIFA World Cup, Coca-Cola sponsored the FIFA World Cup Trophy Tour in which fans were given the chance to see the World Cup trophy. In addition, Coca-Cola provided free entertainment during the tour. K'naan performed 'Wavin' Flag' in 86 countries in 2009 during the FIFA World Cup Trophy Tour and the song became the unofficial anthem of the worldwide event.

This widened and deepened the reach of not only the song and its message of hope and inspiration, but Coke's integral role in bringing this message to a global audience. The promotions had an incredible impact. Because the song's inspirational messages of freedom and togetherness fit so well with people's feelings about this international football match, it was no surprise that the campaign was a huge success. This version of the song reached number one in 17 countries and generated over 800,000 download purchases. The worldwide reach of the track was so immense that it produced a great deal of remixes and covers in different languages across the globe. Remixes and covers appeared in China, France, Greece, Indonesia, Nigeria, Spain and even Thailand. This enormous global response proves that the message of this song connected so deeply with people that they felt the need to recreate and reproduce it in their own languages to share and experience the song with even more people.

It is because of these factors that Seuge says: 'The World Cup with K'naan was so successful from a global perspective that it opened the doors to everything that we are doing today.'

The success of the K'naan campaign, along with all music-centric initiatives, relied on a few extremely important factors, according to Seuge. One of the most important considerations a brand like Coke needs to make when formulating a campaign is the credibility of the artist. For the 'Open Happiness' campaign, this meant choosing an artist who was successful, but shared the youthful spirit and edginess of this teen-focused Coke campaign. 'You are talking about Janelle Monáe and Cee Lo, those people have the edge among this demographic, versus choosing a bigger, household name artist.'

Another marketing effort that centered on music was the 90-minute documentary *Nothing But The Beat* from Burn (a Coca-Cola energy drink brand). The full-length documentary focused on the history and meteoric rise of electronic music and the DJ scene through the eyes of French house music producer and DJ, David Guetta. The film highlighted Burn Energy's brand message of 'inspiring action in those who want to leave their creative mark on the world' (Coke press release[1]) by featuring the influential impact Guetta has had on the international music scene. Seuge explains that this initiative was credible because David Guetta is such a world-renowned artist. He has been a part of the electronic music scene for over 20 years and is therefore the perfect candidate to tell the story of a genre that is currently experiencing an unprecedented rise in popularity.

> The story of Guetta, who has become such an astounding artist that he is worried about losing his credibility, working with us to create a song that tells the history of how he is such a credible underground DJ. Those are compelling stories and that is what drives the conversation.

Nothing But the Beat certainly drove a great deal of conversation, not only about Guetta, but about Burn as well. The documentary was released for free by Coca-Cola's Burn Energy Drink in conjunction with Guetta's label, What a Music, making this initiative the first international free release on iTunes.

After a one-week free period with thousands of downloads, the documentary was made available on YouTube and to date has over 750,000 views. This has resulted in a huge amount of exposure for Burn. News outlets such as *Billboard* and MTV all mentioned the energy drink brand in relation to the documentary. Within six months of the documentary's release, Burn saw its volume sales grow by 25 percent and its Facebook fans increase to over one million. This is a great example of Social Empowerment in practice. By offering its audience easily accessible, stimulating and relevant content that related to – but did not focus on – its product, Coke was able to fuel and be a part of conversations which led to increased exposure for the brand, and ultimately a lift in sales.

Along with artist credibility, the story must also be credible. This was a central concern in Coca-Cola's campaign plans for the 2012

London Olympics. Once again, they wanted to target teens, but, as Seuge says, 'Teens felt disconnected with the Olympics.'

So how does a brand use the Olympics to target a consumer group that does not watch the Olympics? Instead of focusing on the normal Olympic 'story', one of hard work, pay-off and glory that comes with this type of athletic event, Coke decided to focus on the social side of the Olympics. Why? Because that is what teenagers care about.

> So we said, we are going to use music as a way to engage in the Olympics, as a way to get them to pay a little bit more attention to the Olympics. We are also going to show a side of the Olympics that they do not know, which is the social side of the Olympics. Teenagers, they have a normal life, and outside of sports there are a ton of amazing stories that are part of their life and are worth spreading. Therefore, we say all right, how do we merge music into the Olympics?

By zoning in on what teens care about, Coke was able to develop a marketing strategy, and source an artist that helped mold a story that would appeal to this audience. Seuge explains that the target audience came first, then the idea of the story, then the artist. After nailing down these first two aspects, it was easy to find a credible artist that fit the story and appealed to the consumer base. In this case it was British DJ Mark Ronson.

> That is where we say, wow! If we are able to convey the best of the Olympics through the merging of the sound of some music, that would be awesome. So, that was the starting ground that was like, okay so who is the best person to do that? That has credibility in the UK, that is going to be a good ambassador for the London Olympics, but also has credibility to mixing and merging different types of sound. That is where Mark Ronson comes in because he has that credibility. Then, we take Mark Ronson and send him traveling around the world. We capture the sound, we capture the content, and that becomes a credible story. That is what drove the tour of Mark Ronson.

Seuge says that Mark Ronson was the best choice because he was a great fit with the story Coke was trying to tell and the demographic it was trying to target. In this way, Coke chooses its musical partners based not on fame, but authenticity.

> The choice is driven by the credibility of the story. If the story is true and credible with a very established act, great. If the story is credible with a non-established act, great. That is going to be the number one variable.

The last important aspect to consider when developing a music-centric marketing campaign is the relationship between the artist and the brand. This relationship must be based on transparency and shared values. 'Our relationships are about shared values and if we do not believe that there is going to be that shared value, then they are probably not going to work.'

Seuge says that before Coke begins a partnership with an artist, the organization's dedicated music team spends time with the artist, getting to know him or her better, ensure that they not only fully endorse the project, but that they also share Coca-Cola's core company values.

> When we choose the artist, we will make sure the artist believes in what we believe. Therefore, we are going to take the time to talk about what we are as a company, how we work, and how we hope he would want to work with us and make sure he is comfortable with that.

Seuge explains that good relationships are extremely important when attempting to craft a campaign that can resist the test of time. For example, good relationships can lead to follow-up campaigns, which would be easier to develop, and depending on their initial success may lead to a more effective campaign the second time around.

> You have to be conscious that those relationships and that strategy require devotion and nurturing from people at Coke. Our relationship is working right now, because there is commitment on both sides of spending the time to make it work. It is like a marriage. The moment you take it for granted it is gone.

This type of music marketing has been greatly effective for Coke, according to Seuge. From a branding perspective, these types of initiatives are helping Coke tell the right kinds of story to the right groups of people in a way that matters to and connects with them. However, from a sales perspective the numbers are not quite there yet. Seuge has yet to prove that this approach leads directly to increased sales, but he has no doubt in his mind that it soon will. He explains that Coke's sports marketing strategy started as simple sponsorships, but did not translate into a higher sales volume until Coke began actually selling products at these events. Seuge says that once Coke figures out a way to leverage music at a point of sale, the effects will be enormous. 'That is my next big push, how to prove that we are using music to drive volume.'

While it cannot be proven as a 1:1 correlation, it is clear that Coke's music marketing efforts have helped them engage their audiences in a more authentic, meaningful way beyond their product by providing true value and staying connected to the audience they are trying to reach. Rather than being seen as just another soft drink, consumers have come to rely on Coca-Cola to improve their lives by creating unique musical experiences and providing them with content that they feel confident sharing.

CONVERSE

Coca-Cola's employment of Social Empowerment was aimed at recruiting a new generation of teenagers by aligning with more established artists, whose authentic stories would fuel conversations.

It also concentrated on creating unique musical experiences for their consumers to facilitate online sharing, which was a specific way of using Social Empowerment. Brands can also apply the Social Empowerment model, however, to connect more authentically with their target audiences by becoming musical tastemakers and outlets of style leadership that customers can look to and learn from. By introducing their consumers to new artists they would never have found and loved themselves, brands can become involved in conversations that transcend their product. In addition to being providers of new music, brands can connect with their consumers by getting involved at the very ground level through tactics that help artists create music and achieve something they never would have been able to otherwise. This was a central tenet of Converse Rubber Tracks studios.

Unlike Coca-Cola, whose efforts focused on the recruitment of a *new* audience, Converse focused its Social Empowerment efforts on deepening its relationship with, and cementing loyalty among, an *existing* customer base. It is important to note, however, that despite having different objectives for the outcome of these initiatives, both companies fully realized the same thing: that the successful employment of Social Empowerment requires a deep understanding of their target audience's needs, wants and motivations in order to provide experiences that will improve their lives.

Converse is an American sneaker company that specializes in footwear and apparel. They are best known for their creation of the Chuck Taylor All Star sneaker which became immensely popular among subcultures like greasers, punks and skaters throughout the 1970s, 80s and 90s. Woven into the fabric of these subcultures is a deep appreciation for underground, independent music. Recognizing that a need existed among its consumer base, in 2011, the company opened Converse Rubber Tracks, a free recording studio in Brooklyn for independent artists. The 5200-square-foot (483-square-meter) facility supplies musicians with everything they need to record an album, from a practice space, to isolation rooms, a control room, and even recording engineers to facilitate the recording process.

Converse CMO Geoff Cottrill says Converse Rubber Tracks came to fruition because it satisfied some very specific needs of a portion of Converse's consumer base. Cottrill explains that unlike other brands that leverage an artist's image to *seem* cool or relevant to the consumer, Converse focuses its efforts on not seeming cool, but rather, being useful to the consumer. By first understanding who their core consumers are, what they value and what challenges they face, Converse was able to address their needs and improve their lives in a way that reinforces the company's brand identity.

> Brands are searching for equity to borrow from creative people to make them appear to have a certain image or cachet or certain sense of style. There are brands that need to borrow equity. Essentially they say, 'I need you, the artist, to make me, the brand look cool.' And there is a whole lot of that going on. This is okay because it provides opportunity for artists who are smart, to be able to get their content, music and videos out to lots and lots of people, while at the same time helping a brand connect with their consumers. What is different for us is that we actually consider musicians our core consumers. We consider them at the very heart of our consumers.

While other brands use music as a way to target particular consumers by leveraging an artist's image, Cottrill says Converse would not benefit from this type of approach. A large portion of Converse's consumers are musicians to begin with, so the needs of these consumers are different. Cottrill explains that the decline of the music industry puts many independent artists in a difficult position. Major labels no longer have a great deal of capital to invest in up-and-coming artists. Since many labels will not provide the start-up money to record a demo, artists must find a way to record their own and usually even their first couple of albums without any label support. Only after an artist releases music that illustrates his or her commercial viability will a label show interest in bringing them on board. This creates a vicious cycle in which artists need access to quality recording equipment to make good demos so they can get signed. However, they cannot have access to this equipment unless they are already signed to a label. Cottrill and his team listened to and addressed this major frustration of their consumer base.

> So we opened the studio with that in mind saying, 'Look, our core consumer needs our help. Let's do this.' And not with the mindset of, 'Hey, let's borrow some equity from these cool kids so we can make our brand look cool.' Most of these artists are already wearing our product. So this isn't about us recruiting new consumers through giving them experiences in the studio. This is about recognizing existing consumers and deepening the relationship by doing something meaningful for them.

This last idea is paramount to the creation of Converse Rubber Tracks. Sometimes the best marketing does not center on appealing to new customers but rather, finding ways to add value and build deep relationships with current consumers around something they need. In this case, the Converse consumer base was made up of musicians who needed access to recording equipment. Converse listened to this need and created Converse Rubber Tracks. However, catering to this need did not simply benefit Converse consumers with aspirations of becoming professional musicians, it also appealed to the wider Converse consumer base.

> We are fortunate that our core consumers are young, creative people. And as a marketer, once you have that maniacal focus on who your core consumer is you start to do things that connect in a deep and meaningful way with that core consumer group.

So while every Converse consumer may not be a musician, the core base is still comprised of artistic people who value the creation of music. In this way, Converse is appealing to these consumers' creative spirit by aligning the brand with these customers' values. Converse Rubber Tracks does not just appeal to kids who play guitar and need a place to record, it benefits people who appreciate the arts. It is this consumer insight that created a deep consumer connection with the brand and led to the success of Converse Rubber Tracks.

Another important facet of Converse Rubber Tracks is its genuine approach to fulfilling consumers' needs. Artists get to use Converse Rubber Tracks studio for free. Actually, for free. There is no catch. At the end of the recording session the artist owns 100 percent of their music. Cottrill says Converse does not take a cut of the artists' music because it would ultimately hurt the musicians down the line. Many brands would capitalize on owning musical content, viewing it as an opportunity to create a new revenue stream. By focusing on the needs of the consumer, Converse ensures that it will have a long-lasting and meaningful relationship with its customer base that will fuel the longevity of the brand.

> Some brands would say to an artist, 'Okay, we are going to let you record here and all we want in return is to own 10 percent of your content' and there is another band that is in Brooklyn who owns 100 percent of their recordings and copyright. And both bands play at the same bar one night. There are A&R executives from a big label because both of these bands want to get signed. And the label executive loves both bands and talks to the bands and gets down to the nitty gritty on the deal. One of the bands says, 'Listen, I would love to sign this but Converse owns 10 percent of my content.' Chances are the A&R guy is going to go, 'You are not really very profitable for me so I am not going to sign you, I am going to sign the other one.' What has happened there is we have just actually inadvertently prevented them from realizing their dream. So we don't want to own content.

Cottrill says that ultimately if a brand wants to make a truly meaningful connection with the consumer, the brand should not always
expect something in return. Because of this, Converse does not force
musicians recording at Converse Rubber Tracks to wear Converse
apparel or use their social media outlets to post positive things about
Converse. 'We want to get out of people's way so that they can have a
truly meaningful experience with us, remember their experience and
then hopefully continue to develop their careers.'

A couple of years ago, I witnessed first-hand the tremendous
benefits for a brand who took this similar supportive, hands-off
approach with the music community. In 2005, fast-food chain Taco
Bell launched its 'Feed the Beat' campaign to help feed up-and-
coming artists while on tour by supplying them with hundreds of
dollars in Taco Bell gift cards, asking absolutely nothing from the
artists in return. Since the program's inception, the brand has fed
over 600 touring artists. I distinctly remember attending multiple
artist showcases at music industry conferences CMJ and South by
Southwest, during which the artists carved out time from their shows
to express to a packed venue their very heartfelt and sincere gratitude
to the company for their support in the nascent stages of the artists'
careers. There is no traditional advertising budget large enough to buy
that quality of brand equity among a hyper-targeted demographic.

Back to Converse, Cottrill says it is not their goal to help these
artists get famous, and then piggyback on their success. Converse is
simply fulfilling a need they know their customers have: the need to
record. Converse is not attempting to replace record labels, or give
the artists career guidance. They are not taking responsibility for
making the artists who recorded at Converse Rubber Tracks rich and
famous. The brand is providing a service that addresses a specific
need, helping these artists achieve their immediate goals of recording
high-quality music and thereby serving as a first step on their path
to success.

And our thing is like, 'Hey, we are not going to make you famous, we are going to help you record. And if you become famous, we think that's great. We totally do. But if you don't become famous we think that's great. We totally do.' We are kind of indifferent about fame, and it is important to us as a company that our brand reflects that indifference. Don't get me wrong – famous people wear our stuff, but we are not about famous people. We are about all people and the everyday people and like I said before, ten years from now you may be the next Radiohead and ten years from now somebody else who recorded might be a music teacher. Both of them are equally as important to us. We want them to take this memory with them and feelings of goodwill and feelings about Converse with them as they go forward through their life.

From a business perspective this sounds counterintuitive. How can this marketing initiative be successful if there is no hope for a return on the investment? But because of Converse's hands-off, good Samaritan approach, there were positive results for the company, despite the fact that this was not the goal.

What we have learned is by not asking for anything from these artists, that they are being really kind to us in social media and they are saying nice things about us. As a result, our Facebook community has grown tremendously as a result of a lot of these artists saying nice things on our behalf and people becoming fans and joining our page. We are now the number two brand on Facebook behind Coke. Being the number two brand on Facebook behind the world's biggest brand like Coke, we are seeing some pretty good results.

Jon Cohen, CEO and founder of creative advertising agency Cornerstone, helped Converse and Cottrill develop Converse Rubber Tracks. He says that not only has Converse Rubber Tracks helped to put the brand right behind Coke in the number of Facebook fans, but that these fans are extremely engaged, and therefore a huge asset to the brand:

What most people don't realize is Converse has 35 million Facebook friends. The only brand ahead of them is Coca-Cola globally, but with all due respect to Coca-Cola, Converse's 35 million are 500 times more engaged than Coke or anyone else. Fans are putting up pictures of their Chucks. People are talking about their sneakers. There is such passion.

Cohen agrees with Cottrill's assertion that this hands-off approach fosters the growth of an authentic artistic community based on healthy brand–musician relationships. By providing unique value to its consumer base, and not tampering with the artists' creative process, Converse is able to gain some very influential brand ambassadors. Much in the same way that Coca-Cola applied the Social Empowerment model to create personalized musical experiences to encourage sharing among teens, Converse Rubber Tracks provides artists with the tangible value of high-quality recorded music, as well as a unique experience that the participating artists want to share with their social networks.

You know, we can give them resources and the whole idea is those people leave after those couple days at the studio, and they tweet about it, they talk about it, they become unofficial ambassadors for the brand. And we have had 260 bands since June come to the space. So for the investment, which is modest, Converse is getting incredible return on it, incredible mileage. They have an incredible amount of content. They have huge press, huge word of mouth. So it has been a massive success, it really has.

In addition, Converse is receiving a huge amount of positive press from major news outlets since the opening of Converse Rubber Tracks. Cottrill says that the editorial response has been overwhelming. Journalists who love (and hate) Converse are writing positive reviews of the program, which translates into a great deal of positive earned media for the company. *The New York Times*, *Forbes* magazine, *Fast Company* and even *The Wall Street Journal* have written about the studio and Converse in a positive light in the last year.

Because Converse Rubber Tracks has been so successful for Converse, Cottrill says he hopes they will expand the program to pop-up studios at music festivals and other events. This way more artists would have access to the program and Converse could help more people in the music community.

Along with the huge amounts of positive press, Cohen explains that the authentic brand identity that Converse has cemented through the studio has paved the way for many of Converse's future campaigns. For example, Converse worked with James Murphy, André 3000 and Gorillaz to record and produce a song for the launch of the footwear collaboration with Gorillaz. Creating this line-up of ultra-hip, cutting edge artists was not only a huge feat in and of itself, but the fact that Converse was able to get these artists to come together to record a song for an advertisement was unprecedented. It did not just happen because some company asked these artists to do it. It happened because Converse asked these artists to do it. Converse had proved their worth to the music community with Converse Rubber Tracks. By helping struggling members of the artist collective, Converse came to be viewed among members of the community as a credible brand for musicians to partner with. Converse shared these musicians' core values, and because of this, Converse was now able to engage in a new type of music marketing that other brands could not. Converse earned their social capital. Others did not.

> We collectively decided that we are going to start doing these original collaborations. We are going to bring three unique artists together, enable them to record and do something completely outside of their lane, like enable them to do something different than they would in their own recording process. And Converse would have the benefit of giving away a free download, having a visual image that can be in their app home and whatever potential advertising might be.

The response was immensely positive, with publications like *Rolling Stone* and *Pitchfork* giving the song tremendous reviews. But Cohen says that this song would have never been produced if not for the musical credibility Converse racked up with Converse Rubber Tracks. By creating a good rapport with the music community through the creation of Converse Rubber Tracks, these already successful artists felt comfortable doing a Converse advertising campaign. This wasn't simply a case of a brand looking to leverage the artist's credibility for its own benefit. In fact, Converse lent its own credibility and cachet to the artists. As the driver of such a unique campaign and creation of new, great music, Converse helped present the artists as unique and cutting edge just by virtue of its involvement, and therefore became more important than simply the shoes it's selling.

> That is your return on investment now you have their trust. We could not have started that way. The Gorillaz would not have done that. They had trust in the brand, and respect for the other artists who had previously been involved with the brand. So, what I am saying is, it may not be measurable, you know, directly with sales in year one. But as you build the platform, then you can slowly layer in call to action in retail.

But of course we know that nearly everything a brand does in the public eye has fiscal implications. It was revealed during Nike's fourth-quarter earnings call that Converse's signature shoe, the Chuck Taylor All Star, has grown from sales of 4 million pairs in 2004 to 70 million at the close of its 2011 fiscal year in June. So, while brand initiatives like Converse Rubber Tracks cannot be directly linked to a higher sales volume, it is safe to assume that it had a positive effect not only on Converse's brand image, but their sales as well.

Converse Rubber Tracks is not the only example of Converse helping their core consumer base without expecting anything in return.

A few years back, The 100 Club, an iconic punk club in London, was in danger of closing. Converse decided to form a partnership with the venue for three years, helping the club get back on its feet and stay open. There was no publicity about Converse's rescue mission, no brand promotion within the club. Converse did, however, sponsor a few free shows every month for their customers, but once again, the Converse brand was not at the forefront of these events.

> It is about participating in the creative culture and doing something good. As a result, the club has stayed open. The benefit we get is that our consumers continue to have the benefit of the experience of this club being open. We didn't put out a press release. We don't really talk about it that much. It is one of those things we did because we thought it was the right thing to do. As a result, we know all the right people in music, particularly in the London music scene. They know we did it. And we know they know we did it…there is some credibility we get as a result of doing things like that.

Cottrill says Converse's main motive behind initiatives such as Converse Rubber Tracks or saving The 100 Club is not part of an elaborate branding scheme, but rather about doing something useful. Put simply, if you help your consumer achieve something that is important and meaningful to them, you will gain a great deal in return. In fact, when your brand does not expect anything in return, that is when it will gain the most from its consumer base. It's not about sales; it's about your relationship with the consumer.

> Strategically, how are you interacting with your consumer base between purchases? Because that is the time that people decide whether they love you or not. Between purchases. When they might be using your product, but not buying your product.

MOUNTAIN DEW – GREEN LABEL SOUND

With the rise of internet file sharing and music streaming services, the ways in which listeners consume music has changed drastically. Rather than buying an album, someone can just download a track from a torrent site or strip a single off a music blog and put it right into their iTunes library. For consumers, this new model is a fantastic way to experience all kinds of new music for a fraction of what it used to cost. For record labels, the effects were obviously devastating to profit margins and the livelihood of the business as a whole. While labels spent the decade after the rise of Napster trying to return to the good ole' days of platinum record sales and enormous profits, smart brands began to observe these new methods by which consumers experienced music. Using this insight, brands were able to create new, more efficient ways to distribute music, while steering their brand identity and increasing touchpoints with their audiences in the process.

One such smart brand is Mountain Dew. The Tennessee beverage's brand has undergone quite a transformation since its inception in 1954 when the first bottle featured a hillbilly shooting at a government agent fleeing an outhouse – a nod to the drink's origins as a popular mixer for moonshine embraced by bootleggers in the late 1940s. When PepsiCo brought the franchise under its purview in 1964 and consequently launched the beverage into the national marketplace, the company embarked on a series of marketing and advertising campaigns focused on appealing to a wider consumer base before landing on its target demographic.

Between 1966 and 1974, the company's advertising campaigns featured the catchy slogans 'Ya-Hoo, Mountain Dew!', 'Put a Little Ya-Hoo in Your Life' and 'Hello Sunshine, Hello Mountain Dew'. Not long after Mountain Dew began casting its net wider through its marketing activities it was revealed that the soda had found its sweet spot with 18–24-year-old white males interested in an active lifestyle.

With a specific target demographic identified, Mountain Dew's subsequent marketing activities focused on speaking directly to this audience. Most telling of this focus was the launch of Mountain Dew's 'Do the Dew' campaign in 1993. The advertising campaign featured young men performing action-filled, daring stunts such as cliff diving and boogie boarding. Mountain Dew continued to appeal to those consumers seeking a high-octane lifestyle when they began to sponsor the X Games in 1995. The X Games are an alternative, 'extreme' Olympic-type sporting event. But rather than including sports like gymnastics or track and field, the X Games feature sporting events such as BMX, snowboarding, skateboarding, motocross, bungee jumping and even rock climbing. X Games fans were precisely Mountain Dew's target consumer and now Mountain Dew was connecting with them and their adrenaline-seeking lifestyle in ways it never had in the past.

However, in the early 2000s, other energy drink brands began to copy this model. Red Bull, Monster and Vault took similar approaches and sponsored 'extreme' sporting events. Red Bull created the now infamous Flutag competition, where people build their own gliders and attempt to 'fly' off a pier, but ultimately end up diving into a lake. They also bought their own NASCAR and football teams, thus attempting to appeal to the same action-loving consumers that Mountain Dew had locked down. Coke's answer to Mountain Dew at this time was a citrus-flavored energy soda called Vault. In order to compete with Mountain Dew, Vault aired commercials featuring paintball fights and explosions, once again attempting to target the same young, male, daring, active consumer base as Mountain Dew. With so many brands screaming for the attention of the same consumer base, it was extremely hard to get noticed. Because of this, Mountain Dew knew another rebranding was called for.

In an effort to steer the brand away from this increasingly crowded and homogenous carbonated energy drink landscape, Mountain

Dew enlisted the help of creative advertising agency Cornerstone and began exploring new possible directions the brand could take to become more competitive in the marketplace. Their primary challenge now was how to build a brand marketing strategy that enabled Mountain Dew to retain its current consumer base, who they had spent years cultivating and fostering their loyalty, while at the same time attracting an entirely new audience.

By choosing a marketing strategy based in music, Mountain Dew was certain they would not lose their current, sports-oriented consumer base. Since everyone loves music, this approach should not alienate any current customers. It touches everyone, and everything we do. There is not a person on earth that music will not affect emotionally. Music is the one common thread. Music has an impact on almost everything we do. Both actively and passively, it affects fashion, sports and technology, influencing our relationships and the way we experience culture itself.

But that was only the beginning of the important decisions Cornerstone and Mountain Dew had to make to create a successful music-based marketing strategy. As a subset of Pepsi, Mountain Dew traditionally focused marketing dollars on sponsorship models as a way to integrate music into marketing campaigns. High-profile musician sponsorships can produce big results relatively quickly, but the problem is that this model is not sustainable and does not promote longevity. Sponsorships are valuable as long as that deal lasts and media dollars are behind it. Building long-term brand equity through music requires implementing a strategy that first allows for an authentic point of entry into the industry and works to develop trust among the community.

This mentality guided the creation of Mountain Dew's Green Label Sound. Green Label Sound is Mountain Dew's digital singles label, where the brand provides free music to their existing consumers and potential consumers alike. Through Green Label Sound,

Mountain Dew also gives artists access to all the fundamentals a record company should provide: support in making a video, marketing, PR, plus snipes and digital advertising – as well as our expertise. Many indie artists have not been able to get this support, which they need to properly develop, and now Mountain Dew is positioned to make a difference and help further an artist's career.

What it did was to create a hub – the Green Label Sound website – where all of the content can live, and started building a catalog of great music which was made available to traditional places where people discover music. Then it further expanded the footprint beyond the website to encompass live events and national tours.

Through Green Label Sound, Mountain Dew handpicks artists and releases their tracks on the Green Label Sound website for free, thus providing consumers with a quick and easy way to access music that is almost identical to how they discover music on music blogs, with the added benefit of a filtering system that Mountain Dew is able to provide for its consumers because of the brand's laser-like focus on the tastes and passions of its target audience.

In so doing, Green Label Sound is not only keeping up with the times and catering to the current habits of consumers, but also filling a major void left by fallen record label giants and the decaying music industry. In addition to simply releasing the tracks on their blog-based site, Mountain Dew and Green Label Sound also provide the funds for these artists to produce music videos for the single. This is something that no major record labels, and certainly not independent ones, can afford to do any more. Many of the Green Label Sound artists cannot access the capital to produce high-quality music videos or album artwork. There is certainly no chance of them designing any unique platforms by which to build their brand-absent third-party support.

Mountain Dew launched Green Label Sound in the summer of 2008 with tracks from Matt & Kim and The Cool Kids. The initial release gained a great deal of positive response from the press including *The New York Times* and *Rolling Stone*.

The New York Times said Green Label Sound and projects like it could change the music industry in a positive way because 'music deals offered by brands can be fairer and more favorable than traditional label contracts.' Green Label Sound was also featured prominently in an issue of *Billboard* magazine, in which Cornerstone's Co-CEO and Founder, Jon Cohen, appeared on the cover for his revolutionary role in music branding strategy. The magazine called Green Label Sound a 'smart synergy between brand and artist'.

But it was not just the idea of the label that was receiving a positive response. The success of Green Label Sound's artists was also exceptional. Matt & Kim's single, 'Daylight', achieved US Gold status and sold 13,000 copies of their album that featured the Green Label Sound single, according to Nielsen SoundScan. The Cool Kids' video for their single, 'Delivery Man', aired on MTV2 for several months in 2009 and received 4 million YouTube views. The single itself made it into the *Billboard* Top 100 and racked up half a million streams on Last.fm. While the success of these singles was dramatic for Green Label Sound's first few releases, Mountain Dew and Cornerstone did not choose these artists for their potential to achieve fame. Rather, they chose these musicians because they were congruent with the brand's image, and appealed to the musical tastes and passions of the new audience with whom they sought to communicate.

Therefore, the objective of Green Label Sound is to align Mountain Dew with a particular lifestyle. In this case, it is aligning itself with a group of people who are young, music blog surfers who are constantly on the lookout for the next cool, up-and-coming artist. Because of this, choosing the correct artists is particularly important. This target audience is music savvy and consequently interested in many genres.

Green Label Sound artists span several genres including up-and-coming hip-hop acts, electro dance acts and strong indie rock musicians such as The Cool Kids, Matt & Kim, Chromeo and Holy Ghost! – all of whom enjoyed global success as some of Green Label Sound's early signings.

This diversity of genres is not and cannot be picked at random. Rather, if a brand wants to appeal to the consumer base, it is not enough simply to associate a brand with a cool artist; the brand and the marketing initiative must stand for something: they must stand for, and reflect, the culture in which the target consumer lives.

With this principle guiding Green Label Sound, Mountain Dew was able to show its current drinkers it could be organically entrenched in music and the music culture, while still providing the same product that supports their active lifestyle. And more importantly, it showed people that whether they were current or potential consumers, or non-drinkers, the Mountain Dew brand could now spark the powerful thought that: 'Hey, this is a brand that stands for something. This is a brand that is cool. This is a brand that genuinely relates to a culture that I am a part of, or one that I may not consider myself a part of, but can appreciate nonetheless.'

Along with choosing credible artists that appeal to the brand's target customer base, it is also important to foster genuine relationships with the artists in order to create a successful marketing strategy. Without these genuine relationships, it will be difficult for the consumer to believe that the brand is in fact 'cool'. The consumer needs to see that the brand is not exploiting the artists in order to leverage these musicians' images, but rather that the brand's image is truly invested in the well-being of the artists and also entrenched in this particular musical culture.

Mountain Dew has received high praise both from the media and from participating artists in recognition of two features – the program's transparency and the company's willingness to keep the focus on the music. Mountain Dew selected talented, credible artists it believed would continue to grow to the next level, building on the additional resources Green Label Sound was offering. The initiative was honest in its approach and was not simply about finding brand spokespeople – it was about supporting talented musicians and striking up genuinely symbiotic partnerships.

Building trust within the music community is never an easy feat, but this approach is crucial in securing interest from credible artists to participate in wide-scale global brand campaigns. With an authentic foundation of trust guiding the campaign, the response from artists eager to participate in Green Label Sound was tremendous.

But the floodgates did not open simply because Mountain Dew was providing these artists with a platform to release their singles. After all, there are other avenues artists can take to achieve this same goal. It was the relationship Mountain Dew maintained with artists that kept the music community coming back for more. First of all, Mountain Dew and Green Label Sound provided this service without claiming any rights to the artists' music. This is extremely important because it does not discourage potential artists who could be beneficial to the brand from participating in the label. In addition, Mountain Dew does not force artists into promoting their brand at shows, through social media, or in any other ways. If they did do this, the brand would lose its credibility. Consumers are smart. They know when brand promotion is disingenuous and when they detect it, they certainly will not consider that brand cool. Because of this, Mountain Dew decided not to insert the brand in the artists' creative process.

Artists value the fact that Green Label Sound provides them with the fundamentals that have fallen between the cracks in today's record business. Along with the musicians, the biggest winners are music fans (Mountain Dew's target consumers) who get to deepen their experience with their favorite bands.

This credibility is built through not only staying out of the creative process, but providing a helping hand in a way major record labels are no longer equipped to do. For example, when the Brooklyn-based synth-pop duo Holy Ghost! did not have enough money to fund their American tour, they trusted Mountain Dew and Green Label so much that they went to them for help. Green Label ended up financing the tour not because they were gaining a great deal of sales as a result, but because it made the label more genuine, credible and entrenched in musical culture.

Starting a record label that doesn't sell music or generate revenue may seem counterintuitive for a brand whose ultimate goal is increasing its bottom line, not to mention selling soda. But this unique approach has proven effective, especially when you consider the current media landscape.

Because there are so many different ways people interact with advertising today, whether it is on their phone, TV or computer, it is getting harder to reach the consumer. People are so consistently bombarded with information that it is nearly impossible for a brand to be heard in this loud, distracting climate. So brands have to do something that matters. They have to do something that connects with the consumer's lifestyle, something the consumer will remember. And if it truly makes an impact, then it can translate into sales.

What if we could be the people who teach the brands how to embrace this culture, and reach people, and we slowly built a system? And that is not just the crux of how music and brands work. To me, that is also the template for how advertising now works. Advertising is all about attaching something of cultural relevance to what a brand is trying to do, and then figuring out which of the different forms of communication can spread it out there.

Chapter 9

THE FUTURE

IF YOU BELIEVE, AS WE DO, that people will continue to like music and that brands will remain important to our commercial culture, then it is natural that the relationships between music and brands will continue to develop and grow in the years ahead. How they will grow is not yet certain but we can make a few predictions based upon what is already visible.

It is clear that the three silos in the Hit Brand model – **identity, engagement** and **currency** – are already overlapping, and there are good examples of brands that have employed unifying music strategies across the model. Perhaps Disney has the best approach in history to how music can be a part of its corporate identity, play a major role in physical spaces and also generate hard and social currency. Though Disney has not been specifically written up here as a case study, it is well worth a book of its own for how it has owned and developed musical assets for the benefit of the brand across the Hit Brand model.

The emerging field of music branding and associated skills of the music planner would seem to be positioned to drive forward an integrated approach, where the totality of a brand's activities in music across all silos become linked and coherent, cogent and codified. Like Disney, the approaches will likely be based upon brands' understanding that the ownership of assets – NESCAFE's copyrighted notes, Sephora's managed aesthetic or Converse's recording studio – is fundamental to cross-modal music strategies.

Projecting forward, it cannot be too long before we see a brand that owns a major recording artist, their songs and their performances. The idea is an attractive one – the brand using its finance and distribution to make an artist and their output famous. Whether it happens or not will depend upon a further acceptance by audiences that brand 'patronage' is OK and that there's no such thing as 'selling out'. The music is going to have to be great, too, of course.

That this is in the future is almost beyond doubt. There are so many brands seeking to position themselves alongside new and breaking artists that at some stage one of them is bound to hit, and a brand executive (probably one who has read this book) will look into how 360-degree artist deals can be struck.

Of all the corporations in the world most likely to achieve this, Coca-Cola is the one that jumps out. Following its strategic investments in intellectual property owners and distributors such as Music Dealers and Spotify, it is an organization with all the pieces in place to take an emerging artist and sign them to the sort of deal that would see cross-modal music branding around an artist become a reality.

This sort of development will fit into a longer-term trend – the blurring of the distinction between entertainment and branding. The 'branded content' movement, into which one could place the whole idea of Hit Brands, is driving inextricably to a point where direct funding and distribution of entertainment content by brands is the norm, rather than a poor relation to the 'pure' entertainment industry. As it becomes increasingly normal for brands to sponsor and deliver great programming, the concept of brands providing music will simply be accepted by all but the most cynical consumer.

Of course, there is a chance that the sort of 'processed music' that might be produced by a brand – lots of safe themes and a low-risk image – may just be too much junk for people to take. As a rule, audiences do like to feel that the music they consume is natural, organic, fresh and real. Still, everybody loves an occasional bit of fast food and a little bit of processed junk cannot harm. So it really is just a matter of time before a brand like Coke launches and controls the career of a hit recording artist before leveraging the assets – the songs and performance – across its identity, experience and social platforms.

DIMINISHING MARGINAL UTILITY

In our introduction we estimated that around one million new songs are recorded every year. Regardless of the true number, the fact that a lot of new music is made every year is going to have a major impact on the value of, not music as a whole, but any one piece of music in particular. The economic theory of diminishing marginal utility, among other things, would suggest that every new piece of music created is worth a little bit less than the last.

Of course, music is not a homogenous commodity but there are some indications that any individual piece of music will be of diminishing value in the future. Consequently, there is a scenario that says investment in a single piece of new music may generate lower returns than investments in music in general. Perhaps the Coca-Cola investment in Spotify or Apple's cash bonanza with iTunes are early indicators that brands should begin to focus on platforms rather than songs – on the music industry rather than artists.

ON THE SUBJECT OF UTILITY

The future of musical identities almost certainly involves more sounds like the Apple iPhone 'Swoosh' – that is, sounds that have meaning. Going even further, we can start to believe that sounds may even perform functions themselves rather than simply being aesthetically linked to functions. Emerging technologies such as Chirp that use musical phrases as audible character strings, to be heard by smart devices and trigger a function, have recently been launched. It is only a matter of time before these, along with existing technology from the likes of Shazam, will start to add true utility to musical identities.

THE FINAL WORD

Hit brands take many shapes and this book reflects this. The art of creating a hit is still dark, but we hope to have shone a little light on the matter. This book has been created specifically to formalize the idea of music planning – of firmly establishing music as an intentional and successful part of a brand's communications. We seek not only to raise the profile of music for brands, but, in telling some of the stories of how others have created value, we hope we have demonstrated how well-planned and well-executed music strategies can make a real difference to key brand metrics.

Mr Legend Liu, President of the HYX Corporation of China, once told Daniel that there are three types of knowledge. Firstly, we have knowledge of things when we are born. Secondly, we have the knowledge we gain from reading and education. Thirdly, we have the knowledge gained through experience.

You already know that music is important to you – you have known that since you first heard a melody. Book learning – that can only take you so far. Your next step must be to plan and deliver a music strategy. Good luck – here's to having a hit!

NOTES

CHAPTER 1

1. S. Pinker (1997) *How the Mind Works* (New York and London: W. W. Norton & Co.).
2. Apple Press Release: Q1 2011 Unaudited Summary Data, http://techcrunch .com/2013/02/06/charting-the-itunes-stores-path-to-25-billion-songs-sold-40-billion-apps-downloaded-and-beyond, date accessed 11 July 2013. The figure includes apps and video as well as music.
3. D. M. Jackson (2003) *Sonic Branding: An Introduction* (Basingstoke and New York: Palgrave Macmillan).

CHAPTER 4

1. G. Dicum and N. Luttinger (1999), *The coffee book: Anatomy of an Industry from Crop to the Last Drop* (New York: The New Press).
2. http://www.ncausa.org/i4a/pages/index.cfm?pageid=67, date accessed 25 June 2013.
3. http://www.ncausa.org/i4a/pages/index.cfm?pageid=68, date accessed 25 June 2013.
4. http://www.sharpbrains.com/blog/2009/10/24/does-coffee-boost-brain-cognitive-functions-over-time/, date accessed 25 June 2013.
5. http://www.scientificamerican.com/podcast/episode.cfm?id= BD2F8686-0B3F-0458-FA2825CF5B2E71DF, date accessed 25 June 2013.
6. http://www.ncausa.org/i4a/pages/index.cfm?pageid=68, date accessed 25 June 2013.
7. http://www.hoovers.com/industry/coffee-shops/1837-1.html, date accessed 25 June 2013.

8. *The Latte Revolution: World Development* (2002) Vol. 30, No. 7, pp. 1099–1122.
9. http://www.nestle.com/AboutUs/History/Pages/History.aspx? pageId=1, date accessed 25 June 2013.
10. http://en.wikipedia.org/wiki/Nescafé, date accessed 25 June 2013.
11. http://news.bbc.co.uk/today/hi/today/newsid_9622000/9622785.stm, date accessed 25 June 2013.

CHAPTER 5

1. 1. T. Fritz, S. Jentschke, N. Gosselin, D. Sammler, I. Peretz, R. Turner, A. D. Friederici and S. Koelsch (2009) 'Universal Recognition of Three Basic Emotions in Music', *Current Biology*. Leipzig, Germany: Max Planck Institute for Human Cognitive and Brain Sciences.
2. S. Gandhi, M. Mulligan, S. Fowler and L. Wiramihardja (13 January 2010) *US Music Forecast, 2009 to 2014*. Forrester Research Forecast, Recording Industry Association of America.
3. J. Donat (2010) 'MusicMatters + Synovate: Midemnet Global Music Study'.
4. J. Stoneman (2009) 'Marrakesh Records & Human Capital: UK Youth and Music Survey'.
5. G. Brunini and H. Chalmers (2008) *Band and Brands*. WPP and Universal Music Group.
6. P. Callius (2008) *Advertising Avoidance – The Quiet Consumer Revolt*. SIFO Research International.
7. A. C. North, D. J. Hargreaves, and J. McKendrick (2000) 'The effects of music on atmosphere in a bank and a bar', *Journal of Applied Social Psychology*, 30, 1504–1522.
8. R. E. Milliman (1986) 'The Influence of Background Music on the Behavior of Restaurant Patrons', *Journal of Consumer Research*, 13 (September), 286–289.
9. J. D. Herrington (1996) 'Effects of music in service environments: a field study', *Journal of Services Marketing*, Vol. 10 Iss: 2, 26–41.

CHAPTER 6

1. A. North and D. Hargreaves (2008) *The Social and Applied Psychology of Music* (Oxford University Press).

CHAPTER 7

1. R. Peterson and D. Berger (1975) 'Cycles in symbol production: The case of popular music', *American Sociological Review*, 40, 2, 161.
2. *New York Times* (1998) 'Pay-for-Play Back on the Air But This Rendition Is Legal', http://www.nytimes.com/1998/03/31/arts/pay-for-play-back-on-the-air-but-this-rendition-is-legal.html?pagewanted=all&src=pm, date accessed 11 July 2013.
3. *The Economist* (2003) 'The music industry: Upbeat', 30 October 30, http://www.economist.com/node/2177244, date accessed 27 June 2013.
4. D. Goldman (2010) 'Music's last decade', CNN Money 3 February, http://money.cnn.com/2010/02/02/news/companies/napster_music_industry/, date accessed 27 June 2013.
5. http://www.businesswire.com/news/home/20120105005547/en/Nielsen-Company-Billboard's-2011-Music-Industry-Report, date accessed 11 July 2013.
6. P. Resnikoff (2012) 'Drowning? The iTunes store now has 28 million songs...' *Digital Music News*, 25 April, http://www.digitalmusicnews.com/permalink/2012/120425itunes, date accessed 27 June 2013.
7. bandcamp.com.
8. R. Tate (2012) 'Spotify muscles into internet radio, makes Pandora look small', *Wired*, 20 June, http://www.wired.com/business/2012/06/pandora-vs-spotify-infographic/, date accessed 27 June 2013.
9. B. Schwartz (2004) *The Paradox of Choice: Why More Is Less* (New York: HarperCollins); S. S. Iyengar and M. Lepper (2000) 'When choice is demotivating: Can one desire too much of a good thing?' *Journal of Personality and Social Psychology*, 79, 995–1006.
10. http://www.nielsen.com/us/en/press-room/2012/music-discovery-still-dominated-by-radio--says-nielsen-music-360.html, date accessed 11 July 2013.
11. http://pewinternet.org/Reports/2012/Connected-viewers.aspx, date accessed 11 July 2013.
12. eMarketer, January 2012.
13. Paul Simon, 1973.
14. Interview with Seymour Stein on 7 July 2012.
15. D. Richard (2011) 'Music licensing 101', *The National Law Review*, 10 October, http://www.natlawreview.com/article/music-licensing-101, date accessed 27 June 2013.
16. V. N. Salimpoor, M. Benovoy, K. Larcher, A. Daghe, R. J. Zatorre (2011) 'Anatomically distinct dopamine release during anticipation and experience of peak emotion to music', *Nature Neuroscience* 14, 257–262, http://www.nature.com/neuro/journal/v14/n2/full/nn.2726.html, date accessed 11 July 2013.

17. M. Baker (2007) 'Music moves brain to pay attention, Stanford study finds', Stanford School of Medicine, 1 August, http://med.stanford.edu/news_releases/2007/july/music.html, date accessed 27 June 2013.

CHAPTER 8

1. http://216.64.210.4/dynamic/press_center/2011/09/burn-and-david-guetta-movie-premiere.html, date accessed 11 July 2013.

INDEX

Printed and bound in the United States of America